Rhetoric and Reality: Presidential Commissions and the Making of Public Policy

Other Titles in This Series

Westview Special Studies in Public Policy and Public Systems Management

Rhetoric and Reality:
Presidential Commissions
and the Making of Public Policy
Terrence R. Tutchings

Since 1945, the role of the president in shaping domestic and foreign policy has changed dramatically. Though the prodigious growth of the federal bureaucracy under the Executive Branch reflects much of this change, bureaucratic response to the major issues of the past three decades has been ineffective or nonexistent, and a notable parallel development has been the increasing use of public commissions in the policymaking process.

Dr. Tutchings studies more than 100 public commissions using a model of the policymaking process that includes demands, decision and information costs, and policy results and outcomes. Reviewing the results of the commissions as reflected in presidential support of recommendations (via proposed legislation) and in congressional response, he notes that their membership has typically been dominated by government/corporate elites: as this membership has become more pluralistic, there has been a sharp decline in the contributions of the commissions to the policymaking process.

Perhaps the most significant contribution of the book is its detailed development of the concept of rhetorical policy as a first step in the policymaking process.

Terrence R. Tutchings is adjunct professor of sociology at the University of Texas at Austin and executive associate at the Hogg Foundation for Mental Health.

Rhetoric and Reality:
Presidential Commissions and the Making of Public Policy

Terrence R. Tutchings

Westview Press / Boulder, Colorado

*Westview Special Studies in Public Policy
and Public Systems Management*

Copyright © 1979 by Westview Press, Inc.

Published in 1979 in the United States of America by
  Westview Press, Inc.
  5500 Central Avenue
  Boulder, Colorado 80301
  Frederick A. Praeger, Publisher

Library of Congress Cataloging in Publication Data
Tutchings, Terrence R.
  Rhetoric and reality.
  (Westview special studies in public policy and public systems management)
  Bibliography: p.
  1.Executive advisory bodies—United States.
I.Title.
JK468.C7T87   353.09'3   79-12891
ISBN: 0-89158-657-1

Printed and bound in the United States of America

TB 2/17/81

Contents

Figures and Tables

Preface

This book is intended for the use of those teachers and learners who have an interest in the nonroutine workings of the American political system. It does not deal with the hard quantitative measures of dollars and programs, nor with the delayed effects of policy impacts. It does attempt to address some of the personalities, processes, and rhetoric of policy formulators in ways that can predict subsequent actions in the forms of programs and dollars. The goals of the book are to describe presidential advisory commissions—the structure, processes, and results—while emphasizing some differences compared with the more routine policymaking entities; to suggest possible functions of commissions in the American political system; to relate the personalities, processes, and outcomes of these commissions to policies actually put into operation; and to explore the applicability of general models of policymaking in this special case. In no small sense, the present effort seeks to bridge the gap between the rhetoric of promises and the reality of policy that finds its way into action. Hopefully, the book will find an audience with everyone who has an interest in the American political system. Realistically, it is aimed at scholars in the fields of American politics, American society, elites, public administration, political sociology, and those exciting, interdisciplinary efforts made in hope of understanding—and surviving—the "American experience."

The role of the president in shaping national policy is

certainly powerful and perplexing. Along with the powers
granted to that office by the Constitution must surely rank the
personal and political powers of the officeholder. Constitutional, political, and personal powers clash head-on in that
area of national policy concerned with the allocation of scarce
resources, the area of public policy. The needs of the public,
balanced with the limited capability of the government to
provide for those needs, compete for the scarce resources in the
public policy arena.

Paradoxically, the scarce resources have come to include
things that are much less tangible than the use of the word
"resources" would imply: human dignity, law and order, and
educational opportunity are quite difficult to measure in the
commonly used dollar measures of policy analysis. Time is yet
another resource that is scarce when the persistent need for
social equity is met with a deliberate legislative process that
often seems to exacerbate problems in seeking their solutions.
The increasing scale and complexity of the governmental establishment has seen a parallel development in the increasing
use of advisory commissions by presidents during the last three
decades. To many observers, these commissions represent yet
another dilatory mechanism impeding the timely solution of
problems. To others, commissions suggest a usurpation of the
legislative process by the executive branch. Still others see
commissions as a promising, public way to arrive at the goal
of public well-being. In the exercise of his powers, the president can bring together disparate groups of prestigious elite
members to undertake far-reaching studies of issues of national
importance. In the microcosm of a presidential advisory
commission can be found all of the elements of the overarching
political processes and legislative processes—the articulation
of demands by constituency groups, deliberation of and search
for alternative policies, compromise, coalition, and public
policy actions.

As the work for this book began, Robert L. Sutherland,
although terminally ill, gave me inspiration and encouragement. His contribution to my philosophy of the "way things
should be" goes far beyond anything I might be able to put

down on paper. And, as these words are written, my colleagues and I mourn the death of Lou Schneider, short weeks ago. Not even the memory of Lou's booming voice expounding the function of mourning as an aid in the "redintegration of the community" can convince me that our community of scholars and friends will ever be the same without him and Bob Sutherland.

Shortly after the research for this book began, Tom Wolanin's *Presidential Advisory Commissions: Truman to Nixon* was published. My great indebtedness to him is reflected in the pages that follow, and I acknowledge the encouragement he gave in his correspondence with me. Earlier versions of this work were read by Walter Firey, Sheldon Olson, Dave Perry, and Lou Zurcher; I hope that the finished work reflects the quality of their criticisms. Throughout, it has been my good fortune to enjoy the friendship and knowledge of Reymundo Rodriguez, a member of the President's Commission on Mental Health and a colleague at the Hogg Foundation for Mental Health. Other colleagues here who have provided continuing support are Bernice Milburn Moore, Bert Kruger Smith, Charles Bonjean, and Wayne Holtzman. Thomas L. Dye personably endured my interrogation at a recent meeting, and his help has been considerable; other authors and publishers have been equally amiable and cooperative in granting permission for the use of their material. O Z White and Dan Price pointed me in my present direction several years ago. Most of all, I am indebted to Joe Feagin, whose help has been superlative. In spite of the help of all those persons named, errors and shortcomings remain that are mine alone.

Appreciation is due to those persons who aided in the tedious task of coding a seemingly never-ending collection of data: Patricia Bacak, Dorothe Bozza, Carol Brown, Ralph Culler, Jan Hullum, Linda Hultman, and Margaret Meyer. Various improvements of the original manuscript resulted from the consummate skill and patience of Pamala Bockoven, Betty Jones, and Judy Wygle. Technical assistance with bibliographical material and graphic art came from Anita Faubion and Dianne Craig, respectively.

Although I realize that editors shun acknowledgments that display mawkish sentimentality, I ask their forbearance here. Lynne Rienner, executive editor, and Megan Schoeck, copyeditor, have aided me tremendously. Finally, I would be remiss if I did not acknowledge the contributions of my parents, Paul and Maxine Tutchings, and of Sharon and our children, Molly and Amy; they have given me much.

Terrence R. Tutchings

Rhetoric and Reality: Presidential Commissions and the Making of Public Policy

1
The President and Public Policy

Rhetoric and Reality

The rhetoric of the American political system promises much, but the reality of the system is that little appears to change. The rhetoric arises in response to demands made by various constituencies, interest groups, and influential individuals when canny politicians promise to meet the demands. But it is a long way from the rhetoric of promises to the reality of actions. Even the well-intentioned politician faces a tangle of congressional and bureaucratic red tape in getting his or her rhetoric to the point of realization. An intervening step of considerable importance is the step from promises to public policy. For starters, we can consider public policy to be plans for acting in the public interest.[1] Very much in the public interest are human rights that many of us have come to take for granted—the right to education, health care, equal opportunity, law and order, a just government, and human dignity— yet these are things that more and more fall under the purview of the federal government.[2]

How well does the federal government administer programs connected with these public rights? If we believe only a small part of current political rhetoric or of current and recurring news headlines, the answer is "Not well at all." Apparently, billions of tax dollars have been squandered, pilfered, or lost in the past few years. Equally apparent, basic rights of citizens are still inaccessible to large numbers—witness the sad state of the federal government itself as an "Equal Opportunity Employer," the nagging inequities in income and taxation, and the maldistribution of health services. And all of these glaring failures have been reported by agencies of the federal government itself![3] It is apparent that even when good ideas, expressed in the rhetoric, find their way into public policy, they often fall on hard times in the process of implementation, the next step in the policy process. Then comes the question of what effects have been realized "in the public interest" as results of the plans and actions. Finally, if there are no effects—or if there are undesirable, unanticipated effects—are the original plans and actions reviewed and modified?

Grossly simplistic as the above statements might seem, they outline the conceptual framework that should be used most in the study of policy; but rare indeed is the look at policy that includes all of the basic elements.[4] In this book, we will consider the presidential use of policy commissions as one form of response to the demands made upon the political system. This is only a small part of the policymaking process, but a part that captures the essential elements: political demands, response to demands, and the way in which rhetoric becomes a type of reality through policy. To begin, we will explore the various views of public policy, how it comes about, who makes it in general, and the place of the president and presidential advisory commissions in the overall process.

Public Policy—How Public Is It?

There can be no debate about the effects of public policy; they exist clearly in every conceivable facet of American life—education, reproduction, work, leisure, the food we eat, the air we breathe, the water we drink. In terms of public knowledge, however, policy is not public. What it is, how it is made, who makes it, and how it works are not generally known. Usually the first information that reaches the average American citizen is the response of "Sorry, but that's our policy." In other words, it is often difficult to recognize public policy until it is too late to do anything about it.

Policy Action and Inaction

There are many views of what public policy is, is not, does, and does not. Public policy has been defined as the development of new programs; as the actions of new programs and of existing programs; as "just plain words"; as the results of actions; as the absence of programs and actions; and as the effects that result from the absence of planned programs.[5] According to one noted policy scientist, it is so difficult to define policy that we should not even try.[6] However, perhaps the definition of public policy as plans for acting in the public interest can be considered a viable one.

The development of new programs and the strengthening and redirecting of existing programs are policy *actions*. These actions are not policy in and of themselves; they are responses to policy. One kind of policy action, called acquisitive action, is based on the idea that resources—personnel, operating budgets, and facilities—are acquired as an initial step in the implementation of policy. The implementation of policy involves a second type of policy action, called implemental action. To put it loosely, implemental actions "administer" the programs connected with public policy. These actions give dollars, provide services, and regulate access to education, health care, housing, and voting. Obviously, some benefits are tangible, and some are not. Health, educational attainment, housing, and voting can be measured and implemented, but human dignity and happiness—or "life, liberty, and the pursuit of happiness," if you will—are intangible and more difficult to implement. "Just plain words" denotes the third type of policy action, rhetorical action. Talk is cheap, and it appears that much public policy is dissipated in rhetorical action. However, rhetorical actions, acquisitive actions, and implemental actions can have tangible effects, whether the actions occur singly or in the combinations possible. The effects are policy impacts or policy results.[7]

To complicate the issue a bit, it is quite possible that there will be no results at all. There are many such examples: welfare, medical care, education, wages, social participation, political participation, and human dignity evidently do not find their way to all Americans in spite of massive levels of rhetorical, acquisitive, and implemental actions.[8]

There can be policy results, or things that look like policy results, with no policy and with no policy actions. For example, the Selective Service System, the Federal Bureau of Investigation, the Central Intelligence Agency, and the Department of Health, Education and Welfare have spent a lot of time in recent years explaining just how it happened that they were carrying out discriminatory and/or illegal actions. Surely, there was no policy that directed the Selective Service System to draft large numbers of minority-group members so that disproportionate numbers of blacks would die in Vietnam. No public policy directed FBI and CIA agents to violate the civil rights of political dissidents. It is to be hoped that welfare programs did not intentionally set out to drive fathers and husbands from low-income families.

The lack of public policy can be as significant as the existence of policy. If public rights are accessible to all, then there is no need to worry about the policy or even wonder if there is a policy. On the other hand, if the accessibility is woefully inadequate or unequal, then we look for the policy involved. If there is a policy or plan and it is not working, then it should be changed. In the absence of such a plan, we must at least prepare to make one.

How Is Policy Made?

One assumes that public policy is conscientiously made and that lack of policy or lack of successful policy implementation brings about the search for new and better policy. This sounds suspiciously like the democratic method. As Schumpeter asserts, "Democracy is a political *method,* that is to say, a certain type of institutional arrangement for arriving at political—legislative and administrative—decisions."[9] Since a decision can be something other than a plan for acting in the public interest, the making of public policy is not "democracy in action"; rather, policymaking is one type of institutional arrangement for arriving at political decisions. The decisions might be made democratically, and the institutional arrangements might or might not be democratic, but it is enough for now to consider that policymaking is a conscious process that is part of the political process.

Easton proposed a policy model that captures these notions

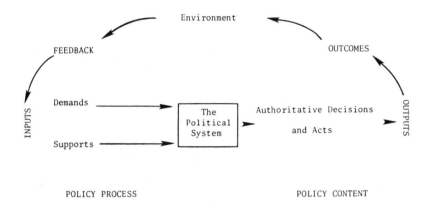

Figure 1.1

EASTON'S POLICY MODEL

David Easton, <u>A Systems Analysis of Political Life</u> © 1965, p. 32. Reprinted by permission of David Easton.

of process and results (Figure 1.1). Proposed in the model is a process of inputs and outputs. Demands, which were mentioned earlier, are made upon the political system. Appropriately or inappropriately, these demands might result in public policy, and the policy might be the cause of policy actions—rhetorical, acquisitive, and/or implemental. The actions might have results, and the results might satisfy the original demands. All of these "mights" are conditioned by the presence and quality of the other elements of the policy model. For example, some demands just do not catch the attention of the political system; other demands are not to be ignored. The supports input consists of information relevant to the demand and relevant to the costs and benefits—tangible and intangible—that are involved with the decisions and acts that compose the policy content's first step, the policy actions. The outputs are the resources directed into acquisition and implementation. The outcomes or results may take place within the environment, or they may fall short of any perceivable change in the environment. The model runs full cycle when the environmental effects, or lack of effects, return as further inputs.[10] Clearly, even with this brief overview, it would be extremely difficult to follow every public policy through such a process.

Salisbury and Heinz propose a policy model that simplifies the view somewhat (Figure 1.2). Their input-output notion is similar to that of Easton, and additionally, their model suggests that a relationship exists among demand, costs, and policy outcome, through the decisional system. However, Salisbury and Heinz indicate that the demands come from a *system*, and Easton's supports are indicated in terms of costs. The characteristics of the demand system, of the decision system, and of the costs involved result in different kinds of policy outcome, according to Salisbury and Heinz.[11] These differing outcomes include the policy actions and results discussed above, and they will be discussed in Chapter 4.

Who Makes Policy?

Who, or what, makes public policy is a tricky question. If the *what* is considered, then the answer could be "the decisional system" or "the political system." More specifically, the answer could be "the president," "the Congress," "the Supreme Court," or "the executive branch." As for the *who*, the decisional system could be anybody; the political system could consist of millions of persons; the president is one; the Congress is hundreds; the Supreme Court is nine, and the executive branch is millions. If we trace the flow of authority in American government from the Constitution, from practice, from legislation, and from judicial decree, we come up with the three branches of the government as the most likely candidates for what and who. Realistically, the place of the Supreme Court is an after-the-fact role, for the most part, although many Supreme Court decisions have certainly attained the status of public policy, especially in the cases discussed above as failure of policy and absence of policy.[12] But a more active role in making public policy is assumed by the president—and the executive branch—and Congress.

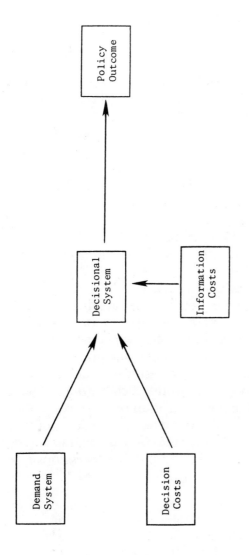

Figure 1.2

SALISBURY AND HEINZ' POLICY MODEL

Robert Salisbury and John Heinz, "A Theory of Policy Analysis and Some Preliminary Applications," in Ira Sharkansky, ed., Policy Analysis in Political Science © 1970. Adapted by permission of Ira Sharkansky.

Continual high interest in the relationship between the executive branch and the Congress is a good indication of the importance of the policymaking roles of initiation, exercise of powers, and limitations of powers. Other areas of study have dealt with the comparative efficacy of each branch of government, usually with the implicit title of "The President *vs.* Congress: Who's Winning?" There are accusations and counter accusations that the president has too much of this and that Congress does too little of that. The president has too much power or too little, as the case might be. The same charges and complaints are made about Congress. These are meaningful questions and answers, which will be discussed subsequently.

For now, the following should be considered: public policy consists of plans for acting in the public interest, public policy is made, and the president and Congress are extremely important in the policymaking process. While this might appear to be an oversimplification, it is actually a strong statement that excludes many of the issues that have confounded public policy's being made public. That is, the actions of agencies in carrying out policies are different from the policies themselves in many instances. Actions without guiding policies present a major problem when the actions are connected with the public interest, and many grave problems in present-day American life are the result of a lack of policy altogether. It is not enough to dismiss social problems with shallow rhetoric or with mere acquisition of resources. Policy that does not do what it should do and policy that does nothing need to be traced to their sources in the governmental structure. The overall workings of the public policy process must be made more public

Or else those who confuse rhetoric with reality, and the plausible with the possible, will gain the popular ascendancy with their swift and simple solutions to every world problem. . . . We cannot expect that everyone . . . will "talk sense" to the American people, but we can hope that fewer people will listen to nonsense (John F. Kennedy).[13]

Crisis and Creativity

The president and Congress have the major responsibility for making policy, but the acquisitive and implemental actions of the federal government center upon the executive branch. The Cabinet-level departments, various offices and councils, and independent agencies (such as the Interstate Commerce Commission and the Federal Reserve Board) comprise the executive branch, and among them, they control the vast majority of the nation's public resources—both physical and intangible. Administratively, these agencies exercise a great deal of control over the private sector as well by way of their regulative functions in trade, fiscal policy, governmental contracting, transportation, education, and a great number of other areas.[14] In addition to the main part of the executive branch, there are over 1,200 tiny, obscure advisory bodies, agencies, task forces, panels, and departments that specialize in minute areas of public policy. For example, the American people have been served by a Tea Tasting Board, by a Condor Advisory Committee, and by numerous other bodies with strange names that collectively comprise what one author has called the "Federal Rathole."[15] Certainly, it is no secret that these agencies of the executive branch and of the "Federal Rathole" constitute the largest bureaucracy in the world.

The advantages and disadvantages of the bureacratic form of organization are well known, or perhaps it is better to say that the disadvantages are generally well known and the advantages are proposed by scientists who study organizations. For complex, routine operations, there probably is no form of organization that can compete with the bureaucracy. By means of bureaucratic procedures, the federal government is able to plan firm budgets and operational plans that range from one year to five years into the future. These complex plans include consideration of the national economy, the world economy, and "likely futures" or possible, future conditions. On the other hand, few of these plans contain much in the way of contingency actions, and most usually assume that the government is in control of its environment.[16]

In terms of the disadvantages of bureaucratic organization, there are a number of things that the government is likely to find itself unable to do with much chance of success. The federal government has been found to be simpleminded in its plans; it apparently operates in only two distinct modes, decision and nondecision; it is inept in dealing with crisis (although it has been found to operate from one crisis to the next with little notice of the crises); and it stifles creativity to the point of nonexistence.[17] If one considers the policymaking process in terms of demands, it is not surprising to find that there are some instances where policy fails and others where policy does not exist. Demands are nasty things for a bureaucracy to confront.

Few demands are made of the Congress as a *congress*. Rather, Congress consists of a gathering of constituencies that can hardly be considered monolithic. Demands made upon the Congress are most often of a parochial nature in those few instances where citizens even contact their representatives.[18] It is the American presidency that is the focal point of demands upon the political system. Perhaps this springs from the symbolic, singular characteristics of the office of the president, established by the Constitution as the *one* whose occupant "shall take care that the laws be faithfully executed."[19] The saying coined by President Truman for his understanding of the office is "The buck stops here." The influence of the president has grown far beyond the constitutional description of the duties of the office and popular perceptions of it. Numerous studies have indicated that the president is the major initiator of public policy and that the presidential influence upon acquisitive actions and implemental actions is considerably greater than the powers exercised by the Congress through appropriations.[20] If any question about the powers of the presidency persists, it is the question of what limits exist. It may be that the major powers of the office depend on the personality and persuasiveness of the officeholder. Whatever the case, demands upon the political system that bear with them charges that the system is not working are challenges to the efficacy of the president as the chief executive officer. It is the president whose popularity rises and falls with the issues of the day. It is the president who makes public statements about the state of the nation and what "the government" intends to do about it. The office of the president is supposed to provide leadership in times of crisis, and "new" and "fair" deals and frontiers raise expectations that something creative is about to unfold from the president's leadership of the government.

One way in which presidents have dealt with crises and calls for creativity has been to increase the size of the executive branch bureaucracy. Another response of both the president and the Congress has been the creation of hundreds of ad hoc commissions to provide expert advice in matters of public policy. Certain of these commissions stand out from the others because they are *public* commissions in many ways.

Presidential Commissions

A great number of the ad hoc, or temporary, commissions created by the Congress and by the president have consisted solely of members of the Congress, congressional staff, and members of the executive branch; moreover, their operations and findings have been kept from the public.[21] Other ad hoc presidential commissions have been created rather routinely for the purpose of settling labor-management disputes. These commissions are empowered either by the Railway Labor Act or by the Taft-Hartley Act, which give discretionary authority to the president in those matters where labor disputes affect the nation's security.[22]

However, well over a hundred nonroutine *and* public commissions have been created since 1945, and these have been of high interest to a number of policy scientists and to other persons as well. These commissions are characterized as corporate groups:

1. created by a public act of the president or of the Congress;
2. which are advisory to the president;
3. whose members are appointed by the president;
4. which are initially ad hoc commissions;

5. with at least one "public member" from outside the
   executive branch; and,
6. which make public reports to the president.[23]

In addition to these definitional characteristics, commissions are highly visible to the public. Their members are prestigious, their actions are broad, and their policy recommendations to the president are made with seeming independence from the president and from Congress.[24] Furthermore, these commissions have been created predominantly to deal with pressing social issues—assassinations, race riots, poverty, equal rights—that should be accommodated by the normal operations of the federal government. Some people have viewed these commissions as attempts on the part of the president to usurp the powers of the Congress, others have cast them in the role of "disinterested advisers" to the president, and others have seen them as mechanisms for delaying action altogether.[25]

An important feature of commissions is that the commissioners themselves are selected from the ranks of the elites of the nation. Of the nearly 1,300 members of the commissions being considered, over 60 per cent were prestigious members of some national elite at the time of their appointment. Keeping in mind that each commissioner is appointed by a president, it should be obvious that the composition of each commission represents a careful orchestration of the elite sectors represented by the members. It will be important to consider the balance among the sectors in analyzing the activities of each commission, as the members will be considered to be links with the demand system and a significant part of the decision system itself.

Thousands of persons have taken part in the proceedings of the commissions as members, staff persons, consultants, and witnesses at commission hearings. Thousands of pages of research findings and testimony have been published to document the commissions' activities. Thousands of policy recommendations have been proposed by the commissions, and hundreds of those recommendations have resulted in administrative changes and legislative changes affecting federal policy actions. Many of the policy actions have brought about real policy results. Conversely, many of the commissions have produced only more rhetoric.

Ninety-five of these commissions have been studied in some detail which gives us the opportunity to apply the models of policymaking that have been proposed earlier. (For a complete list of commissions studied, see Appendix A.) The commissions cover the period of time from the Truman administration through the Watergate upheaval, which is a time frame of high interest in terms of the great social changes that were attempted. Civil rights, governance, world unrest, domestic disturbances, and great technological change are among the hallmarks of the period.

The View From the Top

It has been proposed that policy is made by members of elites, and it has also been proposed that the president's role is stronger than that of any other branch of the government. It has been hinted that democracy might find a special meaning in light of the undertakings of the policymaking apparatuses, and it has been asserted that policy commissions have a prominent role in the overall process. The demand system, decision costs, decision system, and policy outcome elements of Figure 1.2 still require additional consideration, and we begin by proposing that the view from the top should be a broadening vision of the policy process, with special emphasis on the role of the commissions. It would be a false promise to suggest that the policymaking system yields to analytical neatness. Policy commissions do not operate in a neat box—they do not ruminate upon things politic with any sacred wisdom unknown to others, although some of them *appear* to do just that.

First, it should be clear that the federal government is routinely constituted to deal with problems: setting goals, controlling activities, coping with situations that call for change, and gathering and processing information to be used in addressing the other three problems.[26] Some problems are more troublesome than others and outstrip the capabilities of

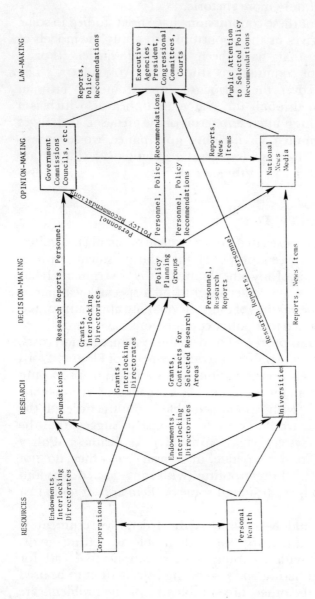

Figure 1.3

THE POLICY PROCESS: THE VIEW FROM THE TOP

Thomas R. Dye, WHO'S RUNNING AMERICA: Institutional Leadership In The United States © 1976, p. 192. Reprinted by permission of Prentice-Hall, Inc., Englewood Cliffs, New Jersey.

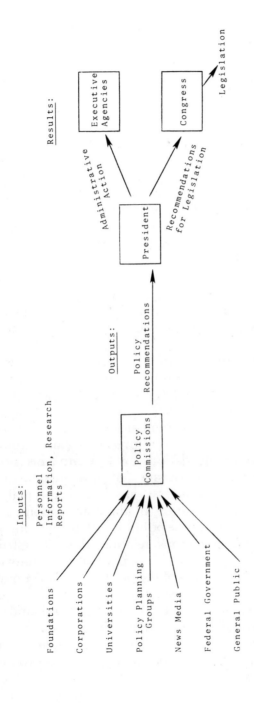

Figure 1.4

IDEALIZED POLICY COMMISSION
PROCESS

the routine operations of the federal government. Commissions often have been the method chosen to formulate policy in these problem areas.

Certainly, there are other avenues that policymaking can follow. One of the most complete maps, drawn by Dye, is reproduced in Figure 1.3. Dye represents policymaking as being under the control of elites, and he enumerates some 5,400 strategic, elite positions that "run" America. He states bluntly that commissions are the "tools" of the elites. Members of these elites mobilize their personal wealth and corporate wealth to serve their own interest; they control research (and the findings); they make the decisions, control the media, and form the opinions that flow into policy and law.[27] This is his "view from the top." However, an emphasis on commmissions alters this view somewhat.

In microcosm, policy commissions capture all of the actors and actions of Dye's policy picture. As shown in Figure 1.4, they draw their commissioners and staff members from among the prestigious and nonprestigious members of corporations, universities, foundations, the news media, other policy planning groups, the government, and from the general public. The actions of the commissions include research and the making of recommendations for policy actions. The suggested view is that the "policy inputs" flow to the policy commissions. From the commission, reports and policy recommendations flow to the president, and from the president, flow recommendations for legislative decisions or administrative actions. It appears that subsequent actions of the president and of Congress are linked to qualitative differences in the composition of the commissions, in the research conducted, and in the policy recommendations made.

In exploring the numerous relationships suggested, we shall rely heavily upon the public reports of the commissions and upon the public records of the president and of Congress. The other main source of information used consists of various biographical references published between 1944 and 1972. Obviously a great deal of decision making goes on behind the scenes, but public information is an important part of public policymaking, and this information can help to explain the complex relationships proposed.

2
The Organizational Dynamics
of Policy Commissions

Demands

Perhaps there is no alternative to the use of commissions,[1] but surely the president and Congress consider other political methods before they decide upon this particular response to demands. Practically all of the commissions studied were created in response to some perceived need or demand that would normally fall within the responsibilities of routinely constituted government agencies. Commissions represent a special kind of response, and it would seem that their structure—commissioners, staff resources, and duration—would indicate some preconceptions on the part of the president concerning the best way to proceed. Furthermore, the amount of information generated or used by each commission and the decisions made by the commission members should reflect differences in demands. The president's staff plays a large part in the selection of commission members and staff, yet the president approves each commissioner appointed, at least in principle. While it is doubtful that a president would appoint an enemy to serve on a commission, it is likely that the public nature of the commission would require at least the representation of some competing constituencies. On the other hand, some of the commissions might well evoke charges of "rubber stamping" because of their low level of activities and rhetorical recommendations.

Creating Commissions

The circumstances that surround the creation of commissions are quite complex. Perhaps the first question that comes to mind is, Why a commission? Different commissions require different answers to this question. Some have been created in response to the requests of significant, elite people. John D. Rockefeller III is purported to have been responsible for the setting up of the Committee on Population and Family Planning (1968-1969). A White House aide interviewed by Wolanin stated: "This Committee was due to the relentless lobbying and intercession of John D. Rockefeller. He beat on the door about once a week on this."[2] Rockefeller himself was appointed cochairman of that commission and Dye discusses in great detail Rockefeller's activities and interests related to population problems.[3] Eunice Shriver, President Kennedy's sister, wielded great influence in the formation of the Panel on Mental Retardation in 1961, and Mary Lasker has been named as the driving force behind the Commission on Heart Disease, Cancer and Stroke in 1964.[4] President Carter created the President's Commission on Mental Health in 1977 because of earlier promises he had made as Governor of Georgia. Reportedly, then-Governor Carter took as a personal affront the closing of mental health programs in his state under the Nixon administration.[5]

Other initiatives for the creation of commissions have been traced to various persons and agencies within the government as well as to private citizens. Interest groups are implicated as well: The NAACP is said to have been the leading advocate of President Truman's Committee on Civil Rights in 1946.[6] Nine of the commissions in this study were created by an act of Congress, and two of those are reported to have been against the president's wishes. According to a White House aide of President Johnson, both the Commission on Marine Science, Engineering and Resources and the Commission on Obscenity and Pornography were "foisted upon" President Johnson.[7] Apparently, the other seven commissions created by Congress were in response to presidential requests for support of the efforts proposed. Whatever the case, the above examples indicate the role of elites in articulating demands to the president and to Congress.

Three of the commissions created could be called responses

to crises: the President's Commission on the Assassination of President Kennedy (1963); the National Advisory Commission on Civil Disorders (1967); and the President's Commission on Campus Unrest (1970). However, "crisis" is a subjective term. In many respects, civil rights, housing, education, welfare, and poverty could be called crisis issues for certain segments of the population, if not for the nation as a whole.

Since the reasons for the establishment of various commissions are themselves varied, two objective indicators of the commissions' beginnings have been selected for distinguishing between high-demand and low-demand commissions: the means of creating and the issue area involved. There is an underlying assumption that the actions of the government are fairly rational and that these distinguishing indicators capture the essence of the demand system.

The first distinction made is that of creation by Executive Order or statute versus creation by a message or letter from the president. All three of the crisis commissions were created by Executive Order, for example. Other, seemingly important, commissions were also created by Executive Order: the President's Committee on Civil Rights (1946), the President's Commission on Migratory Labor (1950), the Advisory Committee on Government Housing Policies and Programs (1953), the President's Commission on the Status of Women (1961), and the President's Commission on Law Enforcement and Administration of Justice (1965) serve as examples. In addition to the commissions mentioned previously that were created by statute, seven other commissions have been created in this way: the President's Committee on Education Beyond High School (1956); the National Commission on Technology, Automation and Economic Progress (1964); and the National Commission on Urban Problems (1965); the National Commission on Product Safety (1967); the Commission on American Shipbuilding (1970); the National Commission on Materials Policy (1970); and, the National Commission on State Workmen's Compensation Laws (1970). Of the ninety-five commissions analyzed, nine were created by statute, and twenty-nine were created by Executive Order. The remaining fifty-seven were created by means of a message, letter, or press release from the office of the president.

Commissions created by Executive Order or statute are considered to be responses to high-demand issues, while creation by other means is taken as evidence of low-demand issues. Although the creation of a commission by any means is likely to indicate that importance is attached to the area in which the commission is to do its work, the distinction drawn is useful.

Table 2.1 shows the number of commissions created by the various means for the five administrations studied. President Johnson created the greatest number of commissions by Executive Order, thirteen; President Nixon created only three in this manner. Eight of the nine commissions created by statute occurred in these latter two administrations. If the means of creating a commission are dichotomized in terms of high demand (creation by statute or Executive Order) and low demand (other means), there exists a strong relationship between means of creation and administration. That is, with the exception of President Johnson, the presidents created more commissions by means other than Executive Order; more recent commissions are significantly more likely to have been created by presidential message or letter ($p = .039$). As can be seen, the significance of this relationship is due mainly to the Nixon administration.

Issue Areas

Another way to distinguish among the various commissions is by means of the areas or tasks assigned for the commissions' attention. Several definitions of "policy area" or issue area were considered, and the "social indicator performance areas" chosen are presented in Table 2.2. According to Gross, these are the areas where the performance of the government can be measured and evaluated.[8] On the basis of the wording of the Executive Order or other documents establishing the commissions, each commission was assigned to one of the areas listed. This is an unavoidably moot process; however, most commissions fit comfortably into only one of the nine categories. Some overlap noticeably, especially in terms of the recommendations made, and we shall return to this point in subsequent chapters. Commissions that were unique, such as the National Advisory Commission on Libraries and the Industry-Government

Table 2.1

NUMBER OF COMMISSIONS BY MEANS OF CREATION BY ADMINISTRATION

Administration	Low Demand	High Demand		Total
	Other	Created by Statute	Created by Executive Order	
Truman	8	0	7	15
Eisenhower	5	1	2	8
Kennedy	7	0	4	11
Johnson	10	5	13	28
Nixon	27	3	3	33
TOTALS	57	9	29	95

$Tau_c = -.199$ $p = .039$

Table 2.2

NUMBER OF COMMISSIONS BY ISSUE AREAS

Area	Number of Commissions
Full employment, fair employment, income, health, social participation, human dignity, the "general welfare"	27
Resource development and conservation	7
Building alliances and international organizations	7
Foreign trade, foreign investment, taxation (tariffs)	4
Immigration, population growth	2
Taxation	1
Conforming with or deviating from law and morality; national constitution and law	7
Advancing and using science and technology; using best possible methods of guiding nation	22
Education	7
OTHER	11

Source: Bertram M. Gross, "The State of the Nation: Social Systems Accounting," in Social Indicators, ed. Raymond A. Bauer (Cambridge: MIT Press, 1966). Adapted with permission from the American Academy of Arts and Sciences.

Special Task Force on Travel, were placed in the "Other" category. The two largest categories represent fairly well the major areas of policymaking activities.

Temporal Variations in Demand

Of course, the administrations of and the commissions appointed by the five presidents studied varied over time, and they varied with the personality and political power of the incumbent. There are, however, important ways in which they seem to remain the same. The most striking similarity is that the issue areas of Table 2.2 are reflected in the policy concerns of each administration. Other similarities and differences are indicated in the tables following. Table 2.3 gives the frequency and duration of commissions by administration. The numbers of commissions created in any single year ranged from none (1948, 1949, and 1957) to twenty in 1969. There was a slight periodicity in the four-year terms as there was an insignificantly larger number of commissions created in the third year of each presidential term.

The duration of the operations of the commissions ranged from 2 to 36 months, with a mean duration of 10.7 months. This distribution is positively skewed, with the mode of shorter-duration commissions dominated by the numerous short-lived commissions of the Nixon administration. Excluding the Nixon commissions, the mean duration of the remaining 66 commissions was 11.9 months. The Eisenhower years are characterized by the smallest number of commissions, 9, and the mean duration of those commissions was 7.1 months. President Johnson's administration averaged 5.4 commissions per year; President Nixon's first term averaged 8.2 per year. Presidents Kennedy, Eisenhower, and Truman averaged 4.2, 1.1, and 2.5 commissions per year, respectively.

Since 1945, commissions have tended to become ever larger in terms of the number of commissioners (Table 2.4). Not only did the Johnson and Nixon administrations have a larger number of commissions, but these latter two administrations also had a predominance of commissions with 11 or more members. Indeed, the largest commission occurred during the Nixon administration; the President's Commission for the

Table 2.3

FREQUENCY AND DURATION OF COMMISSIONS BY PRESIDENTIAL ADMINISTRATION

	Truman	Eisenhower	Kennedy	Johnson	Nixon	Overall
Number of commissions	17	9	12	28	33	99[1]
Average per year of term	2.5	1.1	4.2	5.4	8.2	3.7
Average duration in months	8.7	7.1	12.5	15.1	6.6	10.7

[1]Includes the four commissions with reports unavailable. These are excluded from subsequent tables.

Table 2.4

SIZE OF COMMISSION BY ADMINISTRATION

| Administration | Number of Commissioners | | | |
	3-10	11-15	16-50	Total
Truman	10	2	3	15
Eisenhower	6	0	2	8
Kennedy	8	1	2	11
Johnson	4	10	14	28
Nixon	8	16	9	33
TOTALS	36	29	30	95

$Tau_c = .235$ $p = .006$

Observance of the Twenty-fifth Anniversary of the United Nations included 50 members. Over 1,200 commissioners' names are listed in the commission reports, and the average number of members per commission was 13.6. President Johnson's commissions averaged almost 16 members, while President Truman's averaged around 9 members. The trend toward larger commissions is significant ($p = .006$).

Information Costs

We would expect that relationships exist that link the demand system and issue areas with the level of information costs involved with commission operations. Complex areas and high demand should result in a great deal of fact-finding to aid in decision making. Three characteristics of commissions have been selected to reflect the information costs of the policymaking process: the size of the professional staff, the use of consultants—both individuals and organizations—and the carrying out of scientific research.

Commission Staff

Most of the work is done by the staff members. They prepare briefing documents, collect data, coordinate meetings, and work out differences of opinion among the commissioners.[9] Although twenty-one of the commission reports make no mention of staff members, the other seventy-four name from one to ninety-seven professional staff members. This number excludes persons identified as "students," "clerical," "secretaries," and "typists." Thus, the only persons counted as professional staff are those specifically identified as such. Obviously, the reliability of these data is much lower than that for the number of commissioners; the most likely bias resulting from counting the professional staff members in this way would be that the figures underrepresent the actual number of persons serving as professional staff. This is most pronounced in the reports issued during the Nixon administration; nine of these reports name no staff members, and nine name only one. According to the data presented in Table 2.5, the Johnson administration shows a marked use of staffs with eleven or more professional members, while the other administrations generally indicate staffs numbering ten or fewer. Overall, there is a significant tendency toward *reporting* fewer staff members, at any rate (p = .016). A noteworthy point about the Nixon commissions is that twelve of the twenty-two persons named as staff directors were members of the White House staff.

Consultants

In terms of information costs, neither the number of consulting individuals nor the number of consulting organizations changed significantly over the five administrations. Fifty-one of the reports make no mention of the use of consulting individuals; fifty-six make no mention of the use of consulting companies; forty-four commissions employed from one to over one hundred individuals in consulting roles; and, thirty-nine commissions used the services of from one to over a hundred outside consulting agencies. There was a high association between the use of consulting individuals and the use of consulting organizations (Table 2.6). In general, the use of

Table 2.5

SIZE OF COMMISSION STAFF BY ADMINISTRATION

Administration	Number of Staff Members			
	None, or 1	2-10	11 and over	Total
Truman	3	6	6	15
Eisenhower	2	4	2	8
Kennedy	5	4	2	11
Johnson	2	12	14	28
Nixon	18	9	6	33
TOTALS	30	35	30	95

$$Tau_c = -.201 \qquad p = .016$$

consulting individuals went hand in hand with the use of consulting companies, as almost all the commissions that employed at least one consulting individual also used the services of at least one outside firm. However, two commissions used consulting organizations exclusively: the National Advisory Commission on Libraries contracted with nine private firms (1966-1968), and the President's Commission on an All-Volunteer Armed Force made use of the services of three outside firms (1969-1970). Generally, the higher the number of individuals consulted, the higher the number of firms involved with the commissions' operations ($p < .0001$).

Two points should be noted concerning the reliability of these data. First, since practically all of the commission reports acknowledge contributors, it is unlikely that the data used understate the actual figures. That is, even those commissions that did not employ outside consultants nonetheless acknowledged the contributions of staff members and members of government agencies. Secondly, the outside sources usually

Table 2.6

THE USE OF OUTSIDE CONSULTANTS— BY COMMISSIONS

Number of Consulting Individuals	Number of Consulting Companies				Commission Totals
	0, or 1	2-5	6-9	10 and more	
0	49	1	1	0	51
1-10	12	5	2	3	22
11-20	4	2	1	2	9
21-30	0	0	0	0	0
31 and more	7	3	1	2	13
TOTALS	72	11	5	7	95

Tau = .442 $p < .0001$

contributed data that were incorporated in the text of the commission reports, and the sources of the data were annotated in most instances.

Research

Connected with the use of consultants are the methods used by commissions in information gathering or fact-finding. Some reports made no mention of either outside advice or research. Others documented the involvement of considerable numbers of persons and organizations in developing their findings. In general, five kinds of information gathering were evident in the reports:

1. none reported, or "internal wisdom only" assumed
2. the use of existing studies from other sources, including both the federal and the private sector
3. hearings with witnesses from outside the government
4. new research by the commission staff or by outsiders
5. a combination of new research and public hearings

(It should be noted that a commission was not considered to have conducted new research unless the findings were made public.) Using these divisions, one can roughly determine the efforts expended in acquiring data for the commissions' deliberations.

Naturally, the levels of data gathering reflect the use of individuals and organizations outside of the commissions, for the publishing of newly generated research accompanied the use of outside consultants in many instances. As Table 2.7 shows, forty-one commissions utilized hearings combined with new research—a fairly high number. Eighteen commissions gathered their information through public hearings only; another sixteen made use of new research findings and did not use public hearings. Twenty used only government agency reports created for other purposes or relied exclusively upon knowledge internal to the commission. The six reflecting this latter mode of data gathering were all created during President Nixon's administration, and eight of the fourteen that used existing government reports only were also Nixon commissions.

Actual Information Costs

Unfortunately for a discussion of information costs, virtually no budgetary data exist for the commissions. Furthermore, many of the information-gathering costs are hidden, as most Executive Orders and statutes establishing commissions directed that "all departments and agencies of the Federal Government . . . shall cooperate with the Commission and furnish it such information and assistance, not inconsistent with law, as it may require in the performance of its functions and duties."[10] Most commissions—including those created by presidential message or letter—were funded from the "Emergency Fund for the President" or from a "Special Projects" fund.[11] While the resources available to commissions are not limitless, from one million dollars to over twenty-five million dollars has been available to the president in any year since 1945 for such activities. Indeed, since 1943, a total of 200 million dollars is a conservative estimate of the amount of money that was available.[12] Only one commission depended

Table 2.7

LEVEL OF DATA GATHERING BY ADMINISTRATION

	None Reported (Internal Wisdom)	Existing Data Only	Public Hearings Only	New Research	New Research Plus Hearings	Total
Truman	0	0	9	2	4	15
Eisenhower	0	1	4	2	1	8
Kennedy	0	3	2	2	4	11
Johnson	0	2	2	4	20	28
Nixon	6	8	1	6	12	33
	6	14	18	16	41	95

Tau = -.018   p = .416

entirely upon support from outside the government; the Commission on National Goals was set up by President Eisenhower to operate under the administration of the American Assembly "because of its status as a non-partisan educational institution." The commission was supported by contributions from the Carnegie Corporation, the Maurice and Laura Falk Foundation, the Ford Foundation, the Johnson Foundation, the Richardson Foundation, the Rockefeller Foundation, the Alfred P. Sloan Foundation, and the U.S. Steel Foundation.[13] Initially, President Eisenhower had sought from 3 to 5 million dollars for the operation of this commission, but the final figure contributed was $400,000.[14]

Many of the commissions reported the freely donated services of commissioners, staff members, and advisers along with support from various private and federal sources. However, no dollar amounts are given, and there are usually no budget categories related to research. One exception to this rule was the Commission on Obscenity and Pornography which reported "research . . . in the scholarly and practical communities . . . costing over one million dollars."[15] In short, data on this important variable are not publicly available, if such data exist at all.

Decision Costs

If "politics is the science of the possible and the art of the practical," then we can assume that decision costs consist of the ideological and economic tradeoffs that underlie each decision.[16] These costs defy measurement, and they are obtained here indirectly. In general, the more costly a decision, the more likely it is that not all members of the commission will agree with the decision.[17] While many of the commission reports proclaim virtual unanimity, others indicate more heated disagreement among the commissioners. For example, every one of the ten members of the Commission on National Goals presented dissenting comments in the published report.[18] Eighteen of the twenty-seven members of the Commission on International Trade and Investment Policy appended their dissenting views to the report.[19] Some commissioners have refused to sign the letter of transmittal accompanying the commission findings, and others have dissented more forcefully. For example, Kenneth B. Keating resigned from the Commission on Obscenity and Pornography, supposedly to "become Ambassador to India"; he was replaced by Charles H. Keating, Jr., appointed by President Nixon.[20] Charles Keating dissented vehemently from the commission's findings, even to the point of suggesting a congressional investigation of the commission.[21] His comments concerning the commission report were closely paraphrased in a press release by President Nixon who said, in part, "I have evaluated that report and categorically reject its morally bankrupt conclusions and major recommendations."[22] Most dissenting statements, however, have dealt with only a part of the commission report or with specific recommendations. Because of the public nature of the reports and the association of each commissioner's name with the findings and recommendations presented, it is assumed that any strong reservations about the report produce obvious dissent in one form or another. This does not mean that no differences of opinion occurred in those reports citing unanimity; rather, those reports probably reflect compromise in their published findings. Other reports are not presented as unanimous but bear no indications of dissent; these are different from those specifically presented as being unanimous.

Levels of distinction among those reports presenting dissenting comments and statements are based upon the number of commissioners dissenting. The number dissenting from the commission findings ranged from none (fifty-two cases) to seventeen of the twenty-nine members of the Commission on International Trade and Investment Policy (1970-1971). That commission was among those achieving the lowest coalition in terms of the percentage of members *not* dissenting from the findings, but there were three other commissions where the achieved coalition, indicated by the number of members supporting the complete report, was even lower. Six of the nine commissioners of the President's Commission on Crime in the District of Columbia (1965-1966) added dissenting comments to the report. Ten of the twelve members of the President's Task Force on Economic Growth

(1969-1970) dissented from the findings of that commission. And, as mentioned, all ten members of the Commission on National Goals (1960) made separate statements, dissenting in part from the findings. At the other extreme, fourteen of the commissions explicitly stated that their reports were unanimous. For example, the Presidential Study Commission on International Radio Broadcasting (1972-1973) stated: "We have arrived at unanimous judgments on the cardinal points in this important foreign policy assignment."[23] The Report of the President's Commission on Campaign Costs states that "the members of this Commission come from both major political parties. We also come from several sections of the country. We have brought to our work varied and extensive experience in political finance and many deeply held convictions. We concur unanimously, nevertheless, in the report we now have the honor to submit to you."[24] Another thirty-eight commissions referred to "virtual unanimity" in their findings. Of the total number of commissioners involved in the ninety-five commissions, only 8.2 percent voiced dissent. However, since so many of the reports were without dissenting comments, this relatively small percentage is noticeable.

Not surprisingly, there is a strong relationship between the number of commissioners and the level of dissent; the greater the number of commissioners, the greater the number of them dissenting (p<.001). Also, since the number of commissioners has increased significantly over time, there is a significant relationship between administration and dissent; the more recent the commission, the more dissenters likely to be found in a commission (p = .006). The relationship between dissent and administration, presented in Table 2.8, is significant (p = .008). The more recent the commission, the lower the achieved coalition.

Summary

Several distinct trends have been noted: commissions have become more numerous in recent years, but they seem to be dealing with more or less the same problems; there has been a significant increase in the number of commissioners, but the

Table 2.8

ACHIEVED COALITION BY ADMINISTRATION

Administration	Dissent	No Dissent	Totals
Truman	5	10	15
Eisenhower	2	6	8
Kennedy	2	9	11
Johnson	15	13	28
Nixon	19	14	33
TOTALS	43	52	95

Tau = -.275   p = .008

number of staff members reported has decreased; more of the commissions reported a high level of information gathering; and, along with the trend toward more commissioners, there appears to be a trend toward more dissent on the part of the commissioners.

Table 2.9 illustrates other interesting relationships among the various structural variables and processes used to describe the policy process thus far. Many of the relationships are expected. For example, larger staffs, the use of more consulting companies, and greater expenditures of effort in gathering information—in general, higher information costs—are associated with the high-demand commissions. Less expected, perhaps, is the slight negative association between demand and coalition achieved; high-demand commissions are more likely to be characterized by the presence of dissent. Duration of commission operations indicates a negative association with achieved coalition; the longer the commission operates, the more likely there is to be dissent. It is possible, however, that the number of commissioners is the overriding factor in this relationship. That is, the higher the demand, the longer the

Table 2.9

ZERO-ORDER CORRELATIONS[1] AMONG VARIABLES—STRUCTURE AND PROCESS

	Demand	Administration	Duration	# Commissioners	# Staff	Consultant Individuals	Consultant Companies	Information-Gathering	Coalition
Demand									
Administration	**-								
Duration	****+								
# Commissioners		***+	*+						
# Staff	****+	**-	****+						
Consultant Individuals		****+	****+		****+				
Consultant Companies	**+	****+	****+		****+	****+			
Information-Gathering	****+	****+	****+		****+				
Coalition	*-	***-	**-	**-				**-	

[1]Tau_c or Tau_b, + = positive correlation; - = negative correlation

*p less than .1
**p less than .05
***p less than .01
****p less than .001

commission's duration, the greater the number of commissioners, and the greater the likelihood of dissent. Most remarkably, information costs seem to have no effect upon the reaching of agreement among commissioners, and the increasing disagreement of more recent commissions indicates that the "rubber stamp" image of commissions is questionable.

3
Policy Elites

Who's Who

America is run by elites. There is little debate about this point. Through personal wealth, the giant corporations, foundations, universities, the media, and the government, the powers of elites in the United States far outstrip the powers of the electorate in making decisions and controlling resources.[1] However, as Dye points out, "*systematic* research on national elites is still very exploratory, and there are no explicit guidelines."[2] While this may be the case in general, the elite memberships of presidential policy commissions are somewhat easier to track down because of the relatively short duration of the commissions. In this study, we are not so much interested in the long career of each member as in the specific elite sector that each member can be assumed to represent at the time of his or her appointment.

The primary question of elite membership concerns which segment of the demand system is represented by a member or members. Since the definition of the sample of commissions used in this book requires that at least one member of each commission be "public," it is reasonable to explore the question of *which* public is represented. In order to achieve a national coalition in an important policy decision, a commission should be made up of representatives of the actual—or potential—opposing groups on any crucial issue.[3] A secondary consideration is the prestige of the commission.[4] If a president desires to reflect a high interest in a problem, then it is likely that he will select important people to serve on his commission. Representativeness and prestige are the two principal guidelines for analyzing commissions' memberships.

Who's Who among Commissioners

In order to determine the biographical characteristics of the commissioners studied, a variety of biographical reference works were employed with *Who's Who in America, Current Biography, Who's Who in American Politics*, and *Biographical Dictionaries Master Index* among the references used. The data sought included: each commissioner's position at the time of appointment, each commissioner's sex and ethnicity, and the professional career of each. However, many of the biographical references have changed their standards for inclusion over the twenty-eight year time period of the study, and other references have been in existence for only a relatively short time. For these reasons, *Who's Who in America* was used as the primary reference for both elite membership and prestige; an elite commissioner is defined as one who was listed in *Who's Who in America* the year prior to his being named commissioner. The other references were used to fill in some missing data.

In all, 1,269 commissioners were named in the reports, and Table 3.1 shows the elite sector membership of the total number of commissioners who were elite members at the time of appointment. The sector definitions are taken from Dye's identifications of "5,416 elite positions,"[5] with the addition of the "other" category in the public interest sector which includes physicians, labor leaders, church leaders, state officials, and private citizens.[6] Table 3.2 compares the relative proportions of sector representation in the present sample with Dye's sample. It is readily apparent that the commissioners represent a more-balanced cross section of the three sectors than do Dye's elite members. Many of the commissioners are also members of Dye's elites, and they are named in his lists of "important people." The public interest sector in the present sample is of interest because of the dominance of persons with educational affiliations; 216 of the 318 members representing

Table 3.1

COMMISSIONERS BY SECTOR

Sector	Number of Commissioners
Corporate Sector (Industrial Corporations, Utilities, Communications, Transportation, Banking, and Insurance Industries)	219
Government Sector (Legislative, Executive, Judicial, Military, and Other Government Agencies)	161
Public Interest Sector (Mass Media, Education, Foundations, Law, Civic and Cultural, Other)	424
(Not found in Who's Who in America)	(465)
Total	1,269

the sector were university administrators, professors, or research scientists at the time of their appointment.

The next variable of interest is the representation of various elite groups on the commissions. Once again, Dye's categories have been applied; for this comparison, his three sectors are broken down further into subcategories. Table 3.3 indicates the number of subcategories represented on commissions by at least one prestigious commissioner. The elite members of seventy-seven of the commissions represented three or more of the major subcategories. Only eighteen commissions included elite members representing two or fewer subcategories; four of those commissions had only one subcategory represented, and one, the President's Task Force on the Mentally Handicapped (1969), had no members listed separately in *Who's Who in America*.[7] Interestingly, two of the four commissions with only one elite group represented were created to deal with problems

Table 3.2

COMPARISON OF DYE'S "INSTITUTIONAL ELITES"[1]
WITH THE SAMPLE OF COMMISSIONERS

Sector	Dye's Sample	Present Sample
Corporate Sector	3,572	219
Government Sector	286	161
Public Interest Sector	1,558	318[2]
Totals	5,416	698

[1]Thomas R. Dye, WHO'S RUNNING AMERICA: Institutional Leadership In The United States © 1976, p. 14. Reprinted by permission of Prentice-Hall, Inc., Englewood Cliffs, New Jersey.

[2]Excludes those classified as "other," a category not in Dye's sample.

of education: the President's Panel on Nonpublic Education (1970) and the Committee on Public Higher Education in the District of Columbia (1963). As would be expected, the elite members of those commissions were educators. The National Commission on Product Safety (1967) had only one corporate elite member among its commissioners, but all of the lesser known were from the corporate sector also. The President's Committee to Appraise Employment and Unemployment Statistics (1961) drew all its elite members from institutions of higher education.

It is also interesting to note which sector had more elite representatives (Table 3.4). The corporate elite members outnumbered the other two sectors on twenty-nine commissions, government members predominated in thirteen, and public sector members were the most numerous in thirty-seven of the commissions. Fifteen had a balance between the public sector and one or both of the other two sectors.

Since the chairmen of the commissions can be considered to

Table 3.3

REPRESENTATION OF ELITE SUB-SECTORS[1]

	Number of Sub-sectors Represented						
	1	2	3	4	5	6	7
Number of Commissions	6	12	31	23	15	6	2

[1]Corporate sub-sectors: Industries, Utilities, Communication, Transportation, Banking, Insurance

Public Interest sub-sectors: Mass Media, Education, Foundations, Civic and Cultural Organizations, Law

be "foremost among peers," it is of interest to consider the segments of the population represented by them. Four commissions were chaired by women: Eleanor Roosevelt headed the President's Commission on the Status of Women (1961); Mrs. Haven Smith, national chairman of American Farm Bureau Women, was chairman of the President's Task Force on Rural Development (1969); Miss Virginia R. Allen, a vice-president of a retail chain, was chairman of the President's Task Force on Women's Rights and Responsibilities (1969); and Jeannette Rockefeller, past president of the National Association for Mental Health, was chairman of the President's Task Force on the Mentally Handicapped (1969). No commission was chaired by a member of any minority group; indeed, few minority group members even served as commissioners. Using Dye's sector definitions (Table 3.5), twenty-seven commissions had chairmen from the corporate sector; twenty-two, from the governmental sector; forty, from the public interest sector; and six had chairmen from sectors not included in Dye's definitions. The excluded categories are medicine, religious institutions, labor unions, state governments, and city governments. This latter group included James Doolittle, a "government adviser" at the time of his appointment; heart surgeon Dr. Michael DeBakey; then-

Table 3.4

DOMINANT ELITE SECTORS

	Corporate	Governmental	Public Interest	"Balanced"
Number of Commissions	29	13	37	15

Governor of Kentucky Edward Breathitt; then-Governor of
Illinois Otto Kerner; Mrs. Haven Smith; and Garson Meyer,
who was the chairman of the New York State Commission on
Aging when he was selected as chairman of the President's
Task Force on the Aging (1969).

Given the data concerning the elite members of the
commissions, another measure of importance is that of the
prestige of each commission. This was derived by computing
the percentage of elite members of each commission. On
average, 64 percent of the members of the commissions were
found to be listed separately in *Who's Who in America*; the
range was from none listed (President's Task Force on the
Mentally Handicapped, 1969) to all members named. The
latter group of commissions consisted of the President's
Advisory Panel on Timber and the Environment (1971), the
President's Special Panel on Federal Salaries (1965), the
President's Airport Commission (1952), and the President's
Water Resources Policy Commission (1950).

The influence of the prestige of the commissions and of their
chairmen is indicated in Table 3.6. There is no significant
relationship between the demand system and the number of
prestigious members on the commissions. More recent
commissions are significantly less prestigious, and their
chairmen have been drawn mostly from corporate and
governmental positions. High prestige generally means that
few consulting individuals add their expertise to the proceedings, but prestigious commissions are no more apt to

Table 3.5

SECTOR REPRESENTED BY CHAIRMEN

	Corporate	Governmental	Public Interest	Other
Number of Commissions	27	22	40	6

achieve coalition than the less-prestigious ones. Public sector chairmen seem to foster the achieving of coalition among the members.

It is somewhat surprising that the number of prestigious members on a commission does not reflect the difference between high-demand and low-demand commissions. This effect may be overshadowed by the significant decrease in the prestige of the commissions over the years—elite membership has dropped significantly even though the size of the commissions has grown (p<.0001). Perhaps, the elite membership has declined because the commissions have become more representative. This possibility will be explored in an analysis of the total memberships.

Who Else?

The distinction has been drawn between prestigious commission members and other commission members. Of necessity this is a roughly drawn comparison, but it affords objectivity in assigning prestige scores to commissions. However, as noted in Table 3.1, 465 commissioners were not listed at the time of their appointments in *Who's Who in America*. Other sources provide data on 389 of this number, leaving only 76 "unknown" commission members. As indicated in Table 3.7, the relative proportions of elite and non-elite members are approximately equal for the sectors defined by Dye. In general, the commissioners whose biographies do

Table 3.6

ZERO-ORDER ASSOCIATIONS[1] AMONG COMMISSION VARIABLES

	Demand	Adminis-tration	Consulting Individuals	Coalition
Prestige		****-	****-	
Chairman's Sector		*-		**-

[1]Tau_b or tau_c as appropriate; directions of association as indicated.
 *p < .10
 **p ≤ .05
 ***p ≤ .01
 ****p ≤ .001

not appear in the appropriate edition of *Who's Who* do not seem to be very different from those who are considered more prestigious. As might be expected, they are somewhat younger as a group, and, in the intervening years, many of them have appeared in subsequent editions of the reference work.

Since the proportionate representation of elites and non-elites is so similar, it is of interest to compare the correlations obtained with various structural variables and process variables, treating the elite membership and total membership in turn (Table 3.8). The elite membership shows weak relationships with demand, number of staff members, number of consulting companies, and the level of data gathering. Total commission membership bears more marked relationships with several of the variables of interest. High-demand commissions are significantly more likely to be dominated by the public interest sector, or to have the public interest sector membership balance the governmental sector or corporate sector. High-demand conditions result more often in more public memberships, less likely to be dominated by corporate or government interests. These more public commissions, in turn, are more likely to have larger staffs; are more likely to use

Table 3.7

COMPARISON OF "ELITE" AND "NON-ELITE"
COMMISSIONERS BY SECTOR

	"Elite"	"Non-Elite"
Corporate	219	97
Governmental	161	45
Public Interest	318	134
Other	106	113
Totals	804	389

fewer consulting individuals while undertaking significantly more data gathering; and they are characterized by the significantly higher levels of coalition achieved.

Over the time period of the study, both the elite membership and the total membership have become significantly more corporate. The elites have become more likely to represent corporate or government members. Even though the commissions have become significantly larger, they have become less representative of the various sectors and interests than in earlier years. None of the elite variables is associated with the achieving of coalition. However, since coalitions are markedly less evident in recent years, it is possible that the effects of lower coalition overall mask the effects of membership. There is no difference between high prestige commissions and the others in achieving coalition. Total membership sector dominance is the one membership variable that seems to be associated most systematically with the other variables.

Perhaps the most surprising finding in the analysis of membership is that there exists no overall association between membership and the area of the commission's concerns. In effect, the makeup of a commission does not seem to be tailored for the problem area involved. Whether dealing with urban

Table 3.8

COMPARISON OF ELITE WITH TOTAL MEMBERSHIP[1]

	Demand	Number of Staff Members	Number of Consulting Individuals	Number of Consulting Companies	Data Gathering	Coalition
ELITE MEMBERSHIP						
Sector Representation		*+				
Sector Dominance	*+			*+	***+	
TOTAL MEMBERSHIP						
Sector Representation		*+				
Sector Dominance	****+	****+	**-		****+	****+

[1]Tau_b or tau_c, as appropriate; direction of relationship as indicated

*p ≤ .10
**p ≤ .05
***p ≤ .01
****p ≤ .001
*****p ≤ .001

problems, education, minority rights, law and order, or science and technology, the expertise of the members seems to be an unimportant consideration when compared with prestige or with sector representation. Most likely, the necessary expertise is provided by staff members and consultants, but only fourteen of the staff directors were listed in the biographical references, and a search for information on the hundreds of other staff members and consultants proved to be fruitless.

4
Policy Outputs: Commission Recommendations

Policy Alternatives

Chapters 2 and 3 present data concerning the vastly differing structures, processes, and persons comprising the ninety-five commissions. These differences reflect related differences in the demand costs, information costs, decision costs, and decision systems of the various models of policymaking reviewed. The policy outputs, in this case commission recommendations, should show variability as well. However, since there are at least nine issue areas involved, one would expect that individual recommendations are hardly comparable. In considering policy alternatives, the *types* of policy recommendations made will be of interest,[1] and in dealing with types of policy recommendations, the interest lies with the answers to three questions: Who does "it"? What is "it"? What is the intended result?

Where the federal government is concerned, the prevalent bias seems to be that few alternatives are considered in making decisions.[2] Certainly, few policy decisions are left to private individuals, so the most likely "who" in any analysis of policy types would be the federal government itself. Likewise, the most likely "it" would be regulation of activities by the government. As for the intended result, an obvious one is the definition offered for public policy—action in the public interest. A very rich set of conceptual notions is provided by Salisbury and Heinz (Figure 4.1). Their conceptualization sets out a relationship among the demand system, decision costs, information costs, and the decision system that suggests that

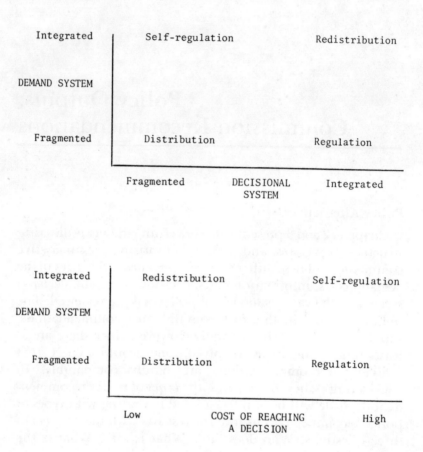

Figure 4.1

POLICY TYPOLOGY

certain types of policy result from certain configurations of the . policymaking system.[3] For example, the "Demand System" is conceptualized as being either "Integrated" or "Fragmented." This distinction has to do with the characteristics of the individuals or entities presenting the demands to the decisional system. A powerful lobby representing the manufacturers of guns and ammunition would represent an integrated demand system; organization, resources, and single-minded organizational goals would be imputed to such a lobby. On the other hand, the statistical aggregate of armed-robbery victims, injuries resulting from the accidental or purposeful discharge of handguns, and the opponents of violence of any form would represent a fragmented demand system. Disorganization, lack of power, and alienation might well characterize such an aggregate. However, one process that is likely to be found within the demand system is that of forming coalitions. Given an issue of sufficient magnitude, it is possible that disparate and individually weak groups might form a coalition strong enough to place demands upon the decisional system. In the same sense, such a coalition could be formed by the decisional system itself. For example, the members of the president's cabinet might put aside internecine differences in an effort to hold together their political party in a struggle with a hostile Congress. It is obvious then that "Demand System" and "Decisional System" are crosscutting concepts that are only analytically separable, at best, for many interests could well be common to both systems and, within the systems, to individuals whose constituencies are broadly based.

As for the policy typology proposed, the following definitions and examples are offered:

- *Redistributive Policy:* Assuming fixed resources, the taking of resources from one population group and allocating these resources to another group defines a redistributive policy. In real-world terms this could be exemplified by a policy that stipulates the reduction of welfare payments to white poverty-level families in order to increase the payments to "double-disadvantaged" minority families.
- *Distributive Policy:* Assuming fixed resources, the

allocating of these resources to all population groups involved defines the aim of a distributive policy. A guaranteed annual wage or an overall tax rebate serve as examples.

- *Self-regulative Policy:* A policy which vests authority in the affected groups or entities is a self-regulative policy. The Supreme Court decision allowing local communities to define obscenity is an example of a self-regulative policy.
- *Regulative Policy:* This type of policy vests authority in a centralized entity. Compared with the community option given in the previous example, a regulative policy would vest authority in a "National Board of Censors."[4]

Clearly, these policy types mix policy actions, intended outcomes, and actors. That is, there could be regulative actions that result in distributive outcomes, or there could be self-regulative actions that have redistributive results.

Rather than restrict the search for policy types to a limited number, the approach used in analyzing the commission reports was to carry out content analysis of the recommendations made, asking the three basic questions posed above, "who does what, and for what purpose." The possible actors range from the president himself to private individuals. Possible actions had to include the rhetorical and dilatory actions of simply "studying the problem" as well as more specific actions. Possible ends range from maintaining the status quo to making significant changes. In all, 5,053 discrete recommendations were located and coded (see Appendix B for a detailed explanation of the process). Table 4.1 (pp. 54-55) shows the coding categories that were developed and used. Actors were assigned numerical codes from 0 to 9, as were actions and ends. For example, a statement that says "Congress should amend PL 89-111" would be coded as "380"—"Congress-change-specific." Unless coded otherwise, congressional actions are legislative actions, so a code of "390" would mean a non-legislative action by Congress with a specific end in mind— such as "congressmen should reduce their staffs." A congressional action with a redistributive end in view, such as

"Congress should pass laws that insure equitable access to education," would be coded as "314," "Congress-enact or legislate-redistributive." "The president should provide moral leadership by employing women in positions of responsibility" would be coded as "159." That the president is the actor is designated by "1," "5" designates a symbolic action, and "9" shows that the end is vague. Because a slight variation in wording could change some codes, notes were added to the codes in some instances. Although there exists the mathematical possibility of one thousand discrete policy types by actor, action, and end, there are realistic limits to the combinations. That is, presidents do not pass laws, but they do propose legislation. Congress would not be likely to call a White House conference; cities do not regulate international trade by legislation. On the other hand, self-regulation could be carried out by any of the actors listed above, and redistribution of resources could be an expected action to be found in a large set of recommendations.

Possible actors include the obvious federal government entities, states, counties, cities, and persons. The categories of actions and ends include the four types suggested by Salisbury and Heinz, along with five others, including symbolic responses. A distinction is drawn between those actions and ends that are "incremental" and those that call for actual, perceivable change.[5] To allow for all possible alternatives, the subcategories of "other" and "specific" types were added.

Alternatives Recommended

Presidential advisory commmissions do not make laws; they do not operate welfare programs, housing renewal programs, or educational programs. Presidential advisory commissions do give advice to the president, and, sometimes, they advise the Congress. This advice is in the form of recommendations, and every commission in the present sample was specifically charged by the president or by Congress to make recommendations. Some of the assignments were general, and some were quite specific:

The Committee shall make a report of its studies to the president

54

Table 4.1

CODING CATEGORIES AND EXAMPLES OF KEYWORDS

	Actors		Actions		Ends
Code	Keywords	Code	Keywords	Code	Keywords
0	Federal and State, Federal and Local Agencies	0	(specific, observable)	0	(specific, observable)
1	President	1	Regulative: enact, prohibit, enforce, legislate, restrict, provide	1	Regulative: control, enforcement, compliance
2	Federal Agencies, Department of...	2	Self-regulative: themselves, independently, own, "according to their decisions"	2	Self-regulative: (same as "actions")
3	Congress, Congressional, Legislative Branch	3	Distributive: all, among, each, allocate, distribute	3	Distributive: (same as "actions")
4	Supreme Court, Courts	4	Redistributive: redirect, equalize, include more, extend	4	Redistributive: equitable, fair, non-discriminatory
5	State, States	5	Symbolic: set example, provide leadership, moral, show the way	5	Symbolic: justice, liberty, freedom, right
6	County, counties, regional governments				

Table 4.1 continued

Actors		Actions		Ends	
Code	Keywords	Code	Keywords	Code	Keywords
7	Cities, Local communities	6	Knowledge/Planning: research, study, plan, develop information, examining	6	Knowledge/Plan: Information, date, research findings, alternatives, methods
8	Person, Individuals, men, women	7	Augment: expand, increase, extend, more, additional	7	Augment: increased capabilities, additional facilities, more services
9	Other ("there should be")	8	Change: Reorganize, establish, create, form, undertake, set up	8	Change: new agency, new program, different way
		9	Other: (vague, unspecified)	9	Other: (vague, unknown)

in writing, and shall in particular make recommendations with respect to the adoption or establishment, by legislation or otherwise, of more adequate and effective means and procedures for the protection of the civil rights of the people of the United States.[6]

The Commmission shall make a report of its studies to the president in writing not later than December 15, 1950, including its recommendations for governmental action, either legislative or administrative.[7]

The Committee shall make, or cause to be made, studies and surveys of the housing policies and programs of the Government and the organization within the Executive Branch for the administration of such policies and programs, and shall advise the Housing and Home Finance Administrator and the president with respect thereto.[8]

The president announced the establishment of the Task Force on Women's Rights and Responsibilities, with Miss Virginia R. Allen, former President of the National Federation of Business & Professional Women's Clubs as the Chairman. The task force will review the present status of women in our society and recommend what might be done in the future to further advance their opportunities.[9]

No commission failed to make recommendations. To be sure, some made only a few, while other commissions submitted literally hundreds. Some recommendations were supported by volumes of research, while others seemingly represented the "expert opinions" of the commissioners. Whether called recommendations or advice, the "policy outputs" numbered from 4 to 260 discrete statements concerning actions to be taken. The mean number of recommendations was 53.1, and the median number was 38.0. A total of thirteen commissions proposed 10 or fewer recommendations; eleven proposed more than 100 recommendations. No recommendation named either a county or regional government as the actor (Table 4.2). The other actors were named in a minimum of .7 percent of the recommendations ("persons" and "courts") to a maximum of 33.4 percent ("federal agencies"). The modal subcategory of actors, "other," is noteworthy in that it comprises 40.5 percent of the total sample.

Table 4.2

FREQUENCY OF ACTORS IN 5,053 RECOMMENDATIONS

Actor	Frequency	Percent
Federal with State and/or Local	410	8.1
President	168	3.3
Federal Agencies	1,690	33.4
Congress	368	7.3
Courts	36	.7
Counties	0	0
States	185	3.7
Cities	118	2.3
Persons	34	.7
Other	2,044	40.5
TOTALS	5,053	100.0

In coding the recommendations, the practice followed was to make note of the "other" subcategory entries, and these are analyzed separately.

The "other" subcategory of actor is comprised of two distinct groupings. The first is "unknown," and over 80 percent of recommendations classified as "actor-other" are of this type. The general form of such recommendations is "there should be" or "it is necessary to. . . ." Clearly, these recommendations deal with some desired state of affairs, but they do not say who is to achieve the ends, and, in many instances, the means of achieving the ends also is unspecified. Of the total number of actors classified as "other," 47 percent are associated with vague actions, and 7 percent are associated with vague or unspecified ends. An example of this phenomenon is the President's Advisory Commission on Universal Training (1947). This commission made seventeen recommendations; sixteen refer to an unknown actor, and the president is named in the remaining recommendation. Moreover, *both* actions and ends are unspecified in eight of the recommendations with an unspecified actor.[10]

The second grouping of "other" consists of actors who are named only one or two times in the total number of recommendations. The best example of this is the President's Commission on Crime in the District of Columbia (1965-1966). Of the 260 recommendations made by this commission, 211 involve specific, but relatively unique, actors: "general counsel," "Prettyman Fellows," "Child Support Section," "Aftercare Program," "the Workhouse," "the Youth Center," "the Good-Time Release Unit," and over seventy other actors are named specifically in the recommendations. In short, this report is very specific in its naming of actors, but the great diversity among the actors named precludes their being classified in any category.[11]

Since 80 percent of the "other" subcategory of actor are vague, and another 11 percent are specific and found in one report, the information loss that appears to be associated with this large subcategory is really quite minimal. We will return to this point later in a discussion of the scoring procedures applied to recommendations.

The high level of involvement of federal agencies is another noteworthy characteristic of the recommendations. Over a third of the actors appearing in the recommendations are the various federal agencies; another 8.1 percent involve federal agencies with other actors at the state and local levels. In many instances, specific federal agencies were named; other recommendations referred to "the appropriate federal agency." Although notes were made of the specific agency named in each recommendation, the information is of little use in light of the great number of combinations of actor, action, and ends possible. That is, the combination of additional subcategories of actors with associated actions and ends adds an additional one hundred possible combinations for each actor named. Generally, the actor named would be the federal agency expected to be involved based upon the area assigned to the commission; for example, housing commissions would be likely to name the Federal Housing Administration, and commissions dealing with the "state of the cities" would be likely to name the Department of Housing and Urban Development. On the other hand, some commissions recommended the involvement of agencies less likely to be involved in the commissions' purported areas of interest. For example, the Advisory Committee on Government Housing Policies and Programs (1953) named a department within the State Department in one of its recommendations; in all, five different federal agencies were named in sixty-eight recommendations made by this commission.[12]

Table 4.3 shows the frequencies of occurrence of the different types of action recommended. Once again, the modal subcategory, "other," reflects vague, unspecified recommendations. Thirty percent of the "actions" recommended were not really actions at all; rather, these recommendations tended to describe some overarching ideal state of affairs—but the means of achieving such states were not recommended. There were, however, a considerable number of recommendations for change. Almost 25 percent of the total recommendations involved reorganizing existing programs or agencies or the establishment of new programs or agencies. This type of recommendation significantly outnumbers the type termed

Table 4.3

FREQUENCY OF ACTIONS IN 5,053 RECOMMENDATIONS

Actions	Frequency	Percent
Specific	139	2.8
Regulative	1,003	19.8
Self-regulative	44	.9
Distributive	56	1.1
Redistributive	29	.6
Symbolic	370	7.3
Knowledge/Plan	394	7.8
Augment	243	4.8
Change	1,257	24.9
Other	1,518	30.0
TOTALS	5,053	100.0

"augment," wherein existing programs or agencies were directed to increase their facilities or levels of services. This finding runs counter to most of the literature that contrasts "incremental change" with more "radical" change.[13] "Self-regulative," "distributive," and "redistributive" actions practically represent "sampling zeros" in the data presented; only 129 of the 5,053 recommendations fell into these three subcategories. As would be expected, perhaps, almost 20 percent of the recommendations called for "regulative" actions; for the most part, these actions combined with a high level of involvement of federal agencies, Congress, and the states as actors.

Table 4.4 lists the frequency of ends in the recommendations made, and several distinct patterns are evident in the findings. For the most part, the ends recommended to be achieved are less

Table 4.4

FREQUENCY OF ENDS IN 5,053 RECOMMENDATIONS

Ends	Frequency	Percent
Specific	1,056	20.9
Regulation	689	13.6
Self-regulation	27	.7
Distribution	315	6.2
Redistribution	239	4.7
Symbolic	276	5.5
Knowledge/Plan	713	14.1
Increase	310	6.1
Change	329	6.5
Other	1,099	21.7
TOTALS	5,053	100.0

vague than are the actors or actions involved. Most striking is the occurrence of specific ends in 20.9 percent of the recommendations. These ends are defined operationally as being observable; a recommendation to make a particular amendment to an existing law would entail a specific, observable end or outcome. Less-specific actions evidently are associated with specific ends, for only 2.8 percent of the actions were deemed to be specifically observable. For example, the recommendation that the "federal government should create two million new jobs" would have an observable outcome, but the means of creating the jobs could entail "urging the private sector" (symbolic), "passing laws" (regulative), or some other subcategory of action.

The various, actual combinations of actors, actions, and ends are quite interesting. Table 4.5 shows the co-occurrences of

Table 4.5

CROSS-TABULATION OF ACTORS BY ACTIONS

Actors	Specific	Regu-lative	Self-Regu-lative	Dis-tribu-tive	Redis-tribu-tive	Sym-bolic	Re-search/Plan	Aug-ment	Change	Other	Total
Combined	1	83	0	3	5	60	37	43	132	46	410
President	3	66	0	1	0	36	4	1	40	17	168
Federal Agencies	32	349	4	35	10	165	149	106	438	402	1,690
Congress	3	223	0	3	1	1	7	2	119	9	368
Courts	0	6	0	0	0	0	0	2	10	18	36
States	0	71	1	0	3	4	9	8	71	18	185
Cities	1	9	2	0	0	4	12	5	48	37	118
Persons	0	5	2	0	2	4	3	0	3	15	34
Other	99	191	35	14	8	96	173	76	396	956	2,044
TOTALS	139	1,003	44	56	29	370	394	243	1,257	1,518	5,053

various actors and actions. Obviously, the most frequent combination of actor and action is "other-other." Another notable joint frequency involving the vague actor involves "change"; however, the most frequent of the actions involving change involve federal agencies. Moreover, the least-likely actions—self-regulative, distributive, and redistributive—are likely to be associated with the "other" subcategory of actor. Practically every one of the ninety cells in the table could be singled out for similar discussion in descriptive terms.

Tables 4.6 and 4.7 show the relationships between actions and ends, and actors and ends, respectively. In Table 4.6, for example, it is obvious that regulative *actions* are associated with regulative *ends*, but they are almost equally likely to involve ends that are specific, redistributive, "knowledge/plan," and change-related. Actions involving change are almost equally likely to involve a changed plan as they are to result in a change of regulatory practices. Table 4.7 indicates that federal agencies are charged with achieving specific ends and with carrying out research or planning with equal frequency.

Since one of the subcategories of actor is null ("counties and regional governments"), the maximum number of cells possible in a three-way cross-tabulation of the types of actor, actions, and ends is 900. The two-way classifications reveal that a total of 36 of the possible 900 cells would be either sampling zeros or structural zeros. This leaves a maximum possible number of 864 three-digit codes in the three-way cross-tabulation; a qualitative indication of the degree of relationship among the three categories—actors, actions, and ends—would be the degree to which the combinations tend to "cluster" within categories of recommendation type. That is, although no satisfactory statistical test exists to test the strength of relationship, the fewer the number of types, the higher the association among the three coding categories.

The combined, three-digit codes of actor-action-end resulted in 390 discrete classifications of policy type. In spite of the preponderance of near-zero cells, 19 of the types contain at least 1 percent of the total number of recommendations; these 19 combinations or categories contain a total of 40.5 percent of the

Table 4.6

CROSS-TABULATION OF ACTIONS BY ENDS

Actions \ Ends	Specific	Regu-lation	Self-Regu-lation	Dis-tribu-tion	Redis-tribu-tion	Sym-bolic	Knowl-edge/Plan	In-crease	Change	Other	Total
Specific	49	42	0	18	4	0	11	3	7	5	139
Regulative	118	200	11	76	107	13	126	84	125	143	1,003
Self-regulative	9	0	6	4	0	0	8	2	13	2	44
Distributive	25	3	0	2	6	0	3	7	0	10	56
Redistributive	2	5	0	5	6	0	1	5	1	4	29
Symbolic	23	22	0	5	13	156	37	1	45	68	370
Research/Plan	42	37	3	15	8	12	127	17	53	80	394
Augment	19	15	0	34	22	5	82	19	9	38	243
Change	151	292	3	121	54	24	230	143	19	220	1,257
Other	618	73	4	35	19	66	88	29	57	529	1,518
TOTALS	1,056	689	27	315	239	276	713	310	329	1,099	5,053

Table 4.7

CROSS-TABULATION OF ACTORS BY ENDS

Actors \ Ends	Specific	Regu-lation	Self-Regu-lation	Dis-tribu-tion	Redis-tribu-tion	Sym-bolic	Knowl-edge/Plan	In-crease	Change	Other	Total
Combined	18	61	1	29	26	38	83	48	24	82	410
President	24	28	0	3	3	31	38	2	17	22	168
Federal Agencies	286	222	3	130	66	91	286	110	104	392	1,690
Congress	47	114	0	27	37	1	33	13	70	26	368
Courts	20	1	0	0	3	0	0	3	0	9	36
States	14	47	3	17	25	1	17	6	17	38	185
Cities	27	21	1	7	7	2	10	10	2	31	118
Persons	5	2	3	1	1	7	3	2	1	9	34
Other	615	193	16	101	71	105	243	116	94	490	2,044
TOTALS	1,056	689	27	315	239	276	713	310	329	1,099	5,053

recommendations. (These categories and percentages are listed in Table 4.8.) While the 1 percent cutoff is rather arbitrary, it points out the small number of categories into which many of the recommendations fall. On the other hand, the fact that nearly 60 percent of the recommendations occurred less than 1 percent of the time points out the great variety of types of recommendations made. It should be noted that the modal subcategories indicate that 15 percent of the recommendations involve actions by federal agencies and that another 2.7 percent involve Congress. That the remaining 22.8 percent can be classified as being "symbolic," "vague," and "nonspecific" serves to underscore the tenor of the commission reports in general: many of the policy recommendations are vague in one way or another.

The major problem with the derived policy types is that the information is dispersed too finely. That is, even if sets of recommendations made by a given commission were to be typed according to the presence or absence of modal types as illustrated above, the resulting categorization of sets would involve a great number of possible combinations. For example, fifteen of the commissions include among their recommendations 20 percent or fewer of the "vague" types of recommendations. Another thirty-six of the reports contain 50 percent or more of this type; no reports exist that do not include some vague recommendations.

Since excluding any category of recommendation type from analysis would result in lower reliability, two alternatives are available to deal with the coded recommendations. The first is to collapse the policy types into a smaller number of categories; the second alternative is to derive a scoring scheme applicable to each recommendation.

Given a table of classifications, there exists a multitude of ways in which to collapse the categories into a smaller number of larger units. The significance of findings resulting from such an operation is as much a characteristic of the way in which the tables were collapsed as it is a characteristic of the data. Although decision rules exist for such operations, they are generally too complicated to result in a meaningful, substantive interpretation of the results.[14] If categories can be ordered according to some underlying dimension, then

Table 4.8

MAJOR CATEGORIES OF RECOMMENDATION TYPES

Code	Description (Actor-action-end)	Percent
210	Federal agency-regulative-specific	1.0
211	Federal agency-regulative-regulation	1.4
219	Federal agency-regulative-other	1.1
280	Federal agency-change-specific	1.3
281	Federal agency-change-regulation	1.6
286	Federal agency-create-research	2.1
289	Federal agency-change-other	1.3
290	Federal agency-other-specific	1.8
299	Federal agency-other-other	3.4
318	Congress-legislate-change	1.2
381	Congress-amend-regulation	1.5
955	Other-symbolic-symbolic	1.1
987	Other-create-increase	1.2
980	Other-change-specific	1.1
981	Other-change-regulation	1.2
966	Other-study-research/plan	1.3
989	Other-change-other	1.6
990	Other-other-specific	9.3
999	Other-other-other	6.0
	TOTAL	40.5

significant relationships among the variables are more valid.
In regard to the three coding categories used with the
recommendations, an underlying dimension of "manipulability" can be assumed.

Political Manipulability: The Possible and the Practical

While rhetorical actions, or policy statements, are a common
coin of the American policy process, dollars are involved in
budgetary actions, in acquisition of resources, and in
implementation of policy. If actions speak louder than words,
then actions also cost more than words. This is the case not only
with dollar costs, but also with the political costs involved in
taking action. Shull has pointed out the need to analyze
variables that are "manipulable by policy-makers."[15] By this he
means that some actions are easier to bring about than are other
actions. For example, Congress might be less likely to take
action on the basis of commission recommendations than
would be the case with federal agencies under the president.
"Manipulability" of the actors and resources involved in the
total policymaking process represents another dimension of
policy. Each subcategory of action can be categorized further in
terms of rhetorical, acquisitive, and implemental actions: the
president says (rhetorical) that Congress (political environment) should provide (appropriate) more money for a certain
agency to increase (agency structure) its services (functional
actions and expenditures). Manipulability strongly suggests
the decision costs of the policy models presented; vastly
different political costs and monetary costs surely would affect
a president's decision on whether to approach Congress or to
change the activities of a federal agency under the executive
branch in order to implement a given policy. Manipulability
further suggests the ends to be achieved, especially the
likelihood of action toward those ends. That is, if the president
directs an agency to do something, then, most likely, it will be
done. On the other hand, if the president *suggests* to the
governors of the states that they integrate the states' schools,
then the hoped-for-outcome is considerably less likely to occur.
    In terms of the actors named in the recommendations, the

Table 4.9

CLASSIFICATION OF ACTORS BY MANIPULABILITY

Rank	Actors (Codes)	
4 (Most Manipulable)	Other	(9)
3	President	(1)
2	Federal Agencies	(2)
1 (Least Manipulable)	Congress	(3)
	Courts	(4)
	States	(5)
	Local Communities	(7)
	Persons	(8)
	Combinations	(0)

notion of manipulability is complementary to the concept of coalition achieved. In effect, those recommendations requiring action on the part of Congress, or on the part of states, are assumed to represent the most "political," hence, least manipulable, actors (Table 4.9). In another sense, those actors represent a greater difficulty to be met in achieving the coalition required to implement the actions and ends, whatever they might be. The same difficulty in achieving coalition is assumed for actions that must be carried out by a combination of federal agencies and other entities at or below the state level, and these actors, too, are in the least-manipulable category. The most manipulable actor is assumed to be no actor at all; the numerous vague and unknown actors mentioned in the discussion of Table 4.2 are of this type. In the middle range of manipulability are the federal agencies and the president himself. Given the president's legal powers as the head of various agencies, it is likely that recommendations made involving federal agencies are more manipulable than those

involving Congress or the states. Finally, those recommendations naming the president are considered to be between federal
agencies and "vague" actors in order of manipulability.

The ordering of categories of actions and ends involves fewer
assumptions; these categories and their respective orders are
shown in Figure 4.2, which follows Shull's typology. Note that
"functional actions" include the nonspecific and symbolic
actions and ends; furthermore, "agency structure" actions and
ends distinguish between "change" and "increase." "Appropriations" includes the distributive and redistributive actions,
and the "political environment" includes legislation and
amending existing laws. Those actions and ends that involve
further research and planning are included as high-manipulability recommendations because, in general, they represent
relatively safe dilatory actions.

On the basis of the ordered categories, four indexes of
manipulability were derived for each commission's set of
recommendations. One index was derived for each category—
actors, actions, and ends—and an overall index was constructed
by combining the three individual categories. For each
recommendation, category weights (from one to four) were
multiplied by the frequency of occurrence of the respective
categories, and the weighted categories were then summed.
Each sum was divided by the total number of recommendations
in that set of recommendations, and the result is an interval-
level metric (Figure 4.3). In addition to the economy gained by
this method of "collapsing" types, there are several other
advantages. For one thing, the scores are reliable in that they
make use of all the recommendations in a given set; possible
unreliability in the assignment of one code to a given
recommendation is diminished by the high reliability of other
assignments, especially in the overall index. Another advan-
tage of the scoring is that it reflects the overall characteristics of
each recommendation set. A score of "1" or "4" indicates that
the recommendations in a set are *mostly* of the antipodal types
necessary for such scores. Scores nearer the midrange of the
metric reflect a mixture of types. The distributional characteristics of the four indexes are given in Table 4.10.

Overall, there are no significant trends over time in any of the

HIGH MANIPULABILITY ←

LOW MANIPULABILITY →

	Functional Actions	Federal Agency Structure or Operations	Appropriations	Political Environment
Actions/Ends: (Rank)	Other, Symbolic Knowledge/Plan	Regulative, Increase	Change, Distributive	Self-Regulative, Redistributive, Specific
	(4)	(3)	(2)	(1)

Figure 4.2

ACTIONS AND ENDS RANKED BY MANIPULABILITY

After Steven A. Shull, "The Relationship Between Budgetary and Functional Policy Actions," in Randall B. Ripley and Grace A. Franklin, eds., Policy-Making in the Federal Executive Branch © 1975. Reprinted by permission of The Free Press.

Recommendation Code		Weights (Manipulability Ranks) (Actor - Action - End)			
	159	3	4	4	11
	380	1	2	1	4
Set 1	248	2	1	2	5
	917	4	3	3	10
		10	10	10	30

Actor Index = 10 ÷ 4 = 2.5
Action Index = 10 ÷ 4 = 2.5
End Index = 10 ÷ 4 = 2.5
Overall Index = 30 ÷ 12 = 2.5

	077	1	3	3	7
	337	1	1	3	5
Set 2	766	1	3	3	7
	977	4	3	3	10
		7	10	12	29

Actor Index = 7 ÷ 4 = 1.75
Action Index = 10 ÷ 4 = 2.50
End Index = 12 ÷ 4 = 3.00
Overall Index = 29 ÷ 12 = 2.42

Figure 4.3

EXAMPLE OF SCORING RECOMMENDATION SETS

Table 4.10

DISTRIBUTIONAL CHARACTERISTICS OF DERIVED INDICES

Variable	Mean	Median	Standard Deviation	Range
Actor Index	2.650	2.683	.608	1.273-4.000
Action Index	3.009	2.882	.426	1.807-3.882
Ends Index	2.699	2.558	.648	1.200-3.778
Overall Index	2.469	2.528	.515	1.258-3.882

indexes; nor are there significant differences among presidential administrations indicated by any of the measures. Examination of the discrete recommendations from which the indexes were derived indicates that none of the components— actors, actions, and ends—have changed in frequency of appearance in recommendations over time. This finding has appeared elsewhere[16] and comes as no real surprise. We must recall that in many instances the recommendations propose alternative courses for governmental action. Action taken is an entirely different issue. Also, the coalition achieved by the members of the respective commissions is related to action taken.

As noted in Chapter 2, agreement among commissioners has declined significantly over time. While there are many plausible explanations for this, informative questions are posed by Dye:

> Do elites in America generally agree about major national goals and the general directions of foreign and domestic policy, and limit their disagreements to the *means* of achieving these goals and the details of policy implementation? Or do leaders disagree over fundamental *ends* and values and the future character of American Society?[17]

By considering the use of commissions as a way for presidents to "feel the pulse of the nation," it is possible to make a cautious, preliminary attempt at answering Dye's questions where commissions are concerned. Relationships among the coalition achieved and the three scales of manipulability reveal there is no relationship between coalition and the policy actors proposed; nor is there any significant relationship indicated with the means of implementation. There is, however, a strong relationship (p = .0008) between coalition achieved and the ends proposed. In general, the more vague and cautious the ends proposed, the more likely a unanimity among the members of the commission. Contrarily, those ends that are specific or that call for change are more likely to provoke dissent.

The next and most important question is what the president and Congress do in response to the recommendations made. The types of alternatives proposed have not varied over time; indeed, they have been more radical than we would expect in calling for administrative change and legislative action. But there is no blatant assumption made that either the president or Congress would take action on a commission's report as a whole. Rather, it is held that such a report would present an overall characteristic tenor of manipulability—or political feasibility.

Policy Results: Presidential Action and Congressional Response

The Next Step

Regardless of what has come before, the presentation of the final report of a commission to the president can be seen as a new demand. The recommendations, dissenting opinions, and supporting evidence in the form of research or testimony represent the expenditure of a significant amount of time and money. The president must decide what to do with the advice given. There are eight possible outcomes in regard to recommendations: either the president supports the recommendations by directing administrative action and/or by supporting legislation, or he does nothing; changes are made in administrative procedures, or they are not made; legislation either is passed or is not passed.

The outcomes, in combination, are condensed in Table 5.1. The combinations are ordered in terms of presidential response, from lowest to highest. Types 1 through 4 include forty-four commissions that met with no presidential support of legislation based on the recommendations made. Twenty-eight commissions resulted in no presidential support, either administrative or legislative, and no legislative action by Congress (type 1). Three resulted in legislation initiated and passed by Congress in the absence of presidential support (type 2; the Air Policy Commission, the President's Task Force on Rural Development, and the President's Task Force on the Aging). The remaining thirteen resulted in adminis-

Table 5.1

COMBINED RESPONSES TO COMMISSION RECOMMENDATIONS

Type	Possible Combinations			Number of Commissions
	President Proposes Legislation	Administrative Action Taken	Legislation Enacted	
1.	No	No	No	28
2.	No	No	Yes	3*
3.	No	Yes	No	13
4.	No	Yes	Yes	0**
5.	Yes	No	No	6
6.	Yes	No	Yes	20
7.	Yes	Yes	No	4
8.	Yes	Yes	Yes	21

* Includes the three instances where Congress initiated and passed legislation without presidential support

** Although there were no combinations of this type, it is a logical possibility in light of types 2 and 3.

trative action only (type 3); and there were no type 4 commissions in the sample. Types 5 through 8 include fifty-one commissions whose recommendations were incorporated in legislation proposed by the president. Six resulted in no legislation (type 5); twenty resulted in legislation with no administrative action (type 6); four, administrative action only (type 7); and twenty-one resulted in administrative action and legislation enacted (type 8).[1] In other words, when the president chose to submit legislation to Congress, he was successful forty-one times in getting some kind of legislation enacted.

To be sure, presidential success in getting congress to pass determine the degree to which the enacted legislation matches the desires of the president. Whatever the case, it is obvious that commission-related legislation proposed by a president has a very good chance of becoming law. Granted that only a small number of presidential initiatives are the result of commission recommendations, it is still instructive to consider the presidential "success" rate for all initiatives during this period of time. From 1948 to 1964, Congress approved 40 percent of the president's initiatives in the domestic area; between 1965 and 1975, 46 percent were passed.[2] The 80-percent rate for commission-related initiatives is comparable to the success rate for defense initiatives during the two periods noted, 73 percent and 61 percent, respectively.[3] Clearly, the commission *method* is quite effective when a president uses it.

In the case of seventy-four reports, the president acknowledged the recommendations with at least an official statement. In another twenty-one instances, the reports either were not acknowledged or were rejected; overall, thirty-one commissions received scant or negative responses to their recommendations on the part of the president (Table 5.2). Two of the commissions created by President Nixon, the President's Task Force on Rural Development and the President's Task Force on the Aging resulted in legislation proposed by Congress in the absence of presidential support.

As indicated, twenty-one of the commission's reports were followed by presidential support and both administrative change and legislation enactment. These are listed in Table 5.3. Once again, the effects of presidential administration are striking, almost to the point of ruling out other effects altogether. However, there are other effects that transcend presidents. For example, the President's Committee on Civil Rights (1946-1947) made recommendations that were part of the civil rights legislation of the 1960s, and the President's Commission on Immigration and Naturalization (1952-1953) saw its findings reflected in the Immigration and Nationality Acts of 1965.[4]

That issue areas change little from one administration to another is evident in the report of the President's Task Force on Women's Rights and Responsibilities, which notes recom-

Table 5.2

COMMISSIONS RECEIVING LEAST POSITIVE PRESIDENTIAL ACTION

President	Commission
Truman	National Commission on Higher Education +Committee to Review Veterans' Hospitals President's Commission on the Health Needs of the Nation Missouri Basin Survey Commission President's Commission on Immigration and Naturalization
Eisenhower	+Commission on National Goals
Kennedy	(None)
Johnson	National Advisory Commission on Technology, Automation, and Economic Progress National Advisory Commission on Food and Fiber +National Advisory Commission on Rural Poverty +*Commission on Obscenity and Pornography National Advisory Commission on Health Facilities +*President's Commission on Income Maintenance *President's Commission for the Observance of Human Rights Year
Nixon	Presidential Task Force on International Development +President's Task Force on Model Cities +President's Task Force On Rural Development +President's Task Force on Women's Rights and Responsibilities +President's Task Force on Higher Education +President's Task Force on Science Policy +President's Task Force on Low Income Housing +President's Task Force on the Aging +President's Task Force on the Physically Handicapped +President's Task Force on Prisoner Rehabilitation +President's Task Force on Urban Renewal +President's Task Force on Highway Safety +President's Task Force on Air Pollution +President's Task Force on the Mentally Handicapped President's Commission on School Finance +President's Commission on Federal Statistics +Commission on American Shipbuilding +National Commission on Materials Policy

+Report not acknowledged, or received negatively by president
*Reports submitted to President Nixon

Table 5.3

COMMISSIONS RESULTING IN PRESIDENTIAL, ADMINISTRATIVE
AND LEGISLATIVE ACTION

President	Commission
Truman	President's Commission on Migratory Labor President's Airport Commission
Eisenhower	President's Commission on Veterans' Pensions
Kennedy	Panel on Mental Retardation President's Advisory Commission on Narcotic and Drug Abuse President's Commission on Registration and Voting Participation
Johnson	President's Commission on the Assassination of President Kennedy President's Commission on Crime in the District of Columbia President's Commission on Law Enforcement and Administration of Justice Commission on Marine Science, Engineering and Resources National Advisory Commission on Selective Service National Commission on Urban Problems President's Committee on Urban Housing National Advisory Commission on Civil Disorders National Commission on Product Safety
Nixon	President's Commission on an All-Volunteer Armed Force President's Advisory Council on Executive Organization President's Task Force on Improving the Prospects of Small Business President's Task Force on Economic Growth Commission on International Trade and Investment Policy President's Commission for the Observance of the Twenty-Fifth Anniversary of the United Nations

mendations made in 1947 by the President's Committee on Civil Rights that had not been implemented at the time of the later report's publication in 1970.[5] In turn, the push for the Equal Rights Amendment in 1979 further underscores the persistence of issues and the relatively slow response of the government in bringing about major changes. More than fifteen years after the Kennedy assassination, debate still surrounds the report of the Warren Commission.

Recommendations and Responses

Although the role of the president in effecting actions based upon commission recommendations is crucial, there still remain eleven instances in which the president has met with legislative rejection of his initiatives and forty instances of no presidential legislative initiative whatsoever. In general, those recommendation sets that involved the less-manipulable actors have been more likely to result in legislative response (Table 5.4). The less-manipulable sets are the ones that frequently name Congress as an actor, and Congress has tended to pass legislation in response to those recommendations. The relationship is significant (p = .021). Although the "riskiest" reports received no legislative response, those sets of recommendations with an actor index of 1.61 to 2.50 were more often followed by legislation. The two commission reports representing the lowest actor index scores were the President's Committee on Civil Rights (1946-1947) and the Commission on National Goals (1960).[6] There are no associations found to exist between the actor index and administrative change or between the actor index and the president's proposing legislation.

There is a significant positive association between the action index and administrative change (Table 5.5). Generally, more-manipulable actions tend to be implemented through administrative means. This finding is reasonable, since the more-manipulable sets of recommendations involve regulation, and many of the regulatory recommendations also involved federal agencies (cf. Tables 4.5 and 4.8). Although the relationship is relatively weak (p = .052), it is borne out further by the relationship between the action index and legislative response

Table 5.4

LEGISLATIVE RESPONSE BY ACTOR INDEX

Response	Actor Index								Totals
	1.10-1.60	1.61-1.90	1.91-2.20	2.21-2.50	2.51-2.80	2.81-3.10	3.11-3.40	3.41-4.00	
Legislation Enacted	0	5	10	10	4	10	0	5	44
No Legislation Enacted	2	3	5	7	8	11	8	7	51
TOTALS	2	8	15	17	12	21	8	12	95

Tau_c = -.238   p = .021

Table 5.5

ADMINISTRATIVE CHANGE BY ACTION INDEX

Change	Action Index							Totals
	1.61-1.90	1.91-2.20	2.21-2.50	2.51-2.80	2.81-3.10	3.11-3.40	3.41-4.00	
Administrative Change	0	2	3	4	7	18	6	40
No Administrative Change	1	6	2	8	15	18	5	55
TOTALS	1	8	5	12	22	36	11	95

Tau$_c$ = .185   p = .052

(Table 5.6). The significant relationship shown to exist between the action index and the legislative response suggests that Congress is generally more likely to pass legislation in response to recommendations for actions that involve change rather than actions that are vague or regulative (p = .025). The commission with the lowest action index was the President's Commission on the Patent System (1965-1966), which proposed fifty-seven recommendations that very specifically defined what the patent system should do, but generally failed to define the actors involved or the ends envisioned. There is basically no relationship between the action index and the president's proposing legislation (p = .356).

Also, there is no relationship between the ends index and the president's proposing legislation or between the ends index and the occurrence of administrative change (p = .237 and .353, respectively). However, once again, there is a significant relationship with congressional response (Table 5.7). In general, the less-manipulable ends are more likely to receive positive legislative response (p = .028). Therefore, even though commission recommendation sets might appear to be quite varied—perhaps even "liberal"—Congress is more disposed to passing legislation as a result of recommendations that involve less-manipulable actors, actions, and ends.

As would be expected, the overall index shows similar relationships (Table 5.8). Viewing the recommendation sets in their entirety, Congress appears to be significantly more likely to respond with legislation to those sets that represent lower political manipulability. Although the "words" do not seem to impress presidents, recommendations appear to carry some weight with Congress, especially when the recommendations are definite.

Nonresponse

It is extremely difficult to single out a reason for the lack of presidential response and Congressional action in those instances where recommendations failed to gain attention. Certainly, there are many possible explanations—and the decision-making operations of the presidents are among the most complex documented[7]—but the problem does not seem to

Table 5.6

LEGISLATIVE RESPONSE BY ACTION INDEX

Response	Action Index							Totals
	1.61-1.90	1.91-2.20	2.21-2.50	2.51-2.80	2.81-3.10	3.11-3.40	3.41-4.00	
Legislation Enacted	0	5	3	7	12	14	3	44
No Legislation Enacted	1	3	2	5	10	22	8	51
TOTALS	1	8	5	12	22	36	11	95

Tau$_c$ = -.225   p = .025

Table 5.7

LEGISLATIVE RESPONSE BY ENDS INDEX

Response	Ends Index								Totals
	1.10–1.60	1.61–1.90	1.91–2.20	2.21–2.50	2.51–2.80	2.81–3.10	3.11–3.40	3.41–4.00	
Legislation Enacted	6	2	3	10	5	7	10	1	44
No Legislation Enacted	4	1	4	5	8	12	8	9	51
TOTALS	10	3	7	15	13	19	18	10	95

$Tau_c = -.224$ $p = .028$

Table 5.8

LEGISLATIVE RESPONSE BY OVERALL INDEX

	Overall Index								
	1.10-1.60	1.61-1.90	1.91-2.20	2.21-2.50	2.51-2.80	2.81-3.10	3.11-3.4	3.41-4.00	Totals
Legislation Enacted	1	7	12	6	11	5	2	0	44
No Legislation Enacted	2	5	7	7	14	9	4	3	51

$Tau_c = -.231$ $p = .024$

lie with the commissions in many cases. Although any selection of recommendations from among the great number made must be biased, it is interesting to sample some of those made by commissions which failed.

Health care remains a concern of the American people. Rising costs, maldistribution of services, and a host of other problems are noted in the newspapers on a daily basis. In 1952, the report of the President's Commission on the Health Needs of the Nation said in part: "We set as a goal for this Nation a situation in which adequate health personnel, facilities, and organization make comprehensive health services available for all, with a method of financing to make this care universally accessible."[8] Among its 123, more specific, recommendations are suggestions that "Federal loans be made to local organizations desiring to institute prepayment plans associated with group practice, for the purpose of encouraging the establishment of group practice facilities;"[9] that "industry give greater consideration to the relation of working conditions to health;"[10] and that "research be given top priority in expenditure of resources for mental illness."[11]

In the area of immigration, the President's Commission on Immigration and Naturalization recommended in 1953:

The Commission believes that our present immigration law should be completely rewritten.[12]

The national origins quota system should be abolished.[13]

The grounds for deportation of aliens already in the United States should bear a reasonable relationship to the national welfare and security; not be technical or excessive; not be retroactive so as to penalize aliens for acts which were not prohibited when committed; and not require the deportation of aliens who entered the country at an early age, or those who have been residents for such a long period as to become the responsibility of the United States.[14]

In 1960, the president's Commission on National Goals stated in part;

The paramount goal of the United States was set long ago. It is to guard the rights of the individual, to ensure his development, and to enlarge his opportunity.[15]

Every man and woman must have equal rights before the law, and an equal opportunity to vote and hold office, to be educated, to get a job and to be promoted when qualified, to buy a home, to participate fully in community affairs. These goals, which are at the core of our system, must be achieved at all levels.[16]

The president's National Advisory Commission on Rural Poverty made broad recommendations in its report of 1967:

That the Federal Government take more vigorous action to reach the goals of the Employment Act of 1946.[17]

That more resources be devoted to measuring and keeping track of the effects of monetary and fiscal policy, particularly the differential effects on various regions, industries, occupations, and population groups.[18]

That the United States Government stand ready to provide jobs at the national minimum wage, or better, to every unemployed person willing and able to work.[19]

We note that in 1952 the President's Materials Policy Commission advised that shortages of natural gas and gasoline could be expected in 1975, and recommended a "comprehensive energy policy" to aid in conservation and to decrease reliance upon imported resources.[20] In response to this, President Truman directed the National Security Resources Board "to undertake a continuing review of the entire materials situation."[21] Yet, in 1973, the National Commission on Materials Policy recommended that "research and development projects for conversion of coal to oil and gas be expedited aggressively, so that they may be able to contribute to our energy needs as soon as feasible."[22]

The cited recommendations, like so many others, do appear to be long on rhetoric and short on specificity. They are somewhat radical as well and serve to remind us of the inherent problem of policymaking: it deals with ideas that are simple to state but exceedingly complex to implement. Yet, those who expound the "costs" of action and implementation should consider equally the cost of inaction highlighted by the examples above. Still, it should be recognized that policy results are not solely a matter of having a president echo the appropriately worded recommendations to an eager Congress.

Many factors are related to subsequent political decisions, whether administrative or legislative.

Complexity

Before turning in the next chapter to a plea for a simplification of the policymaking process, it is appropriate to attempt an interim summary of the relationships explored thus far. Table 5.9 summarizes the findings reported in the first five chapters, and, although we cannot summarize all of the findings in words, we can follow roughly a scenario of demands, information costs, decisions, and responses.

Demands

As discussed earlier and as indicated in Table 5.9, the rough distinction between those commissions created by means of Executive Order or statute and those created by other means is of some importance in relationship to other concerns. The high-demand commissions indicate generally higher levels of effort in terms of duration, staff size, data gathering, and the number of recommendations made. They are slightly more likely to be dominated by elite members and non-elite members from the public sector. High-demand commissions are not more favored by presidential response or legislative action, but they do show a slight tendency toward resulting in administrative change.

Information Costs

These costs reflect the higher level of demand, larger staffs, and more frequent use of consultants. Commissions with greater, public elite-sector dominance tend to do more fact-finding. Policy outputs, or number of recommendations, and policy results—presidents' responses, administrative changes, and legislative actions—are generally greater with higher information costs. However, these costs seem to have negligible effects on the types of policy recommended. Only minor effects are evident from the use of consultants and consulting companies: generally, less-manipulable recommendations are associated with this form of information cost. A greater amount of information has a positive effect on presidential response.

Table 5.9

ZERO-ORDER ASSOCIATIONS[1] AMONG VARIABLES

	Demand	Administration	Duration	Number of Commissioners	Number of Staff Members	Consultants	Companies
Demand							
Administration	a-						
Duration	d+						
Number of Commissioners		c+	a+				
Number of Staff Members	d+	b-	d+				
Number of Consultant Individuals			d+		d+		
Number of Consultant Companies	b+		d+		d+	d+	
Level of Data-Gathering	d+		d+		d+	d+	
Number of Dissenters	b+	c+	b+	b+			
Achieved Coalition	a-	c-		b-			
Issue Area							
Number of Recommendations	b+		d+	b+	c+	a+	b+
Presidential Response		c-		a-	a+		a+
Administrative Change	a+		b+		d+	a+	
Legislative Action		b-					
Overall Index						a-	a-
Actor Index							b-
Actions Index					a+		
Ends Index							
Elite Representation		b-		d+	a+		
Elite Sector Dominance	a+						a+
Prestige		d-				c-	
Overall Representation				d+	a+		
Overall Dominance	c+	c-			c+		
Chairman's Sector		a-					

[1]
< .10 = a
≤ .05 = b
≤ .01 = c
≤ .001 = d

[2]Chi-square values.

Data-Gathering	Dissenters	Coalition	Issue[2]	Recommendations	Pres. Response	Administrative	Legislative	Overall Index	Actor	Action	Ends	Elite Rep.	Elite Dom.	Overall Rep.	Overall Dom.	Chairman's Sector
c+																
b+	a−															
c+				c+	d+											
a+					d+	a+										
						b−										
						b−	d+									
					a+	b−	c+									
		d+				b−										
					a+		a+									
b+		c+							a+							
					b−	c+		b+						a−		
					a+											
		c+	b+											a+		
		b+		b+	a−											

Decision Costs

Assuming that decision costs are related to the coalitions achieved within the commissions, only the number of dissenters appears to have any association with presidential response. As would be expected, more dissenters signal lower presidential attention to recommendations. Coalition is more likely to occur in the more public commissions and in those whose chairman is from the public sector as well. The strongest indicator of coalition involves the ends recommended. Higher coalition is significantly associated with the more-manipulable ends proposed. Disagreement accompanies specificity of recommendations.

Policy Outputs and Policy Results

The resulting sets of recommendations are relatively independent of the process and structure of the commissions. There are a few, weak effects of the size of the staff and the use of outside consultants. However, there are strong, systematic effects shown by all indexes of manipulability on subsequent legislative actions. Recommendations that name Congress as an actor and that call for change as opposed to incremental adjustments seemingly move Congress to favorable action. Still, the president is the key to legislation.

A Final Word on Complexity

Even after applying a variety of statistical controls to the elements of the policy system, independent effects of the information costs, recommendation types, presidential response, and legislative action are evident. To be sure, the president is the link between commissions and policy results, but the numerous instances of legislative lethargy are explained somewhat by the information costs and by the types of recommendations proposed. It is surprising that issue area and demand do not have any noticeable effects upon recommendations made and actions taken, except for a slight effect of high demand in making administrative change more likely. Perhaps the time lag in moving from rhetoric to reality explains the lack of demand effects, and the sweep of recommendations suggests that the issues involved are broader than the scope of commissions' activities.

Two Models: One of Rhetoric and One of Reality

Rhetoric

In Chapter 4, the kinds of words that typified various recommendations were discussed in light of considerations of manipulability, or political feasibility. It was noted that the kinds of recommendations made did not vary over time; only the responses of the president and of Congress seemed to change during the period under study, as indicated in Chapter 5. Moreover, the ambitious nature of recommendations made is somewhat surprising, since the general expectation is that policy maintains the status quo, or at most, calls for a small amount of change in limited areas. Little association was found between demand, information costs, and the types of recommendations made. This calls for more investigation.

Salisbury and Heinz propose a "fundamental hypothesis" for their policy typology (Figure 4.1): "The more costly it is to organize the requisite coalition on an issue, the more likely it is that the policy outcome will be structural rather than allocative."[1] This suggests that the more-manipulable recommendations made would be more likely to receive support from the president, and would be more likely to result in legislation. That is, in the present sample of recommendations, nearly all of the more-manipulable recommendations called for regulation, or were, in the words of Salisbury and Heinz, "more abstractly formulated and more ambiguous."[2] Before considering policy results—presidential, administrative, and legislative response—the policy outputs, or recommendations, should be considered in light of this "fundamental hypo-thesis."

Since it has been demonstrated that there exists a slight negative association between the demand system and coalition and a significant positive association between coalition and the ends index, it is possible to test Salisbury and Heinz's hypothesis contrasting regulative policy with all other types of recommendations (Table 6.1). That is, all other things being equal, do the demand system and the decisional system have any effect upon the type of policy recommended? The regulative policy sets are those that contain mostly regulative recommendations and ends, based upon dichotomizing the overall index of policy. Considering the complete recommen-dation sets of the commissions, there is no difference in the relative occurrence of regulative policy and non-regulative policy controlling for demand and coalition. As Table 6.1 indicates, the sets of recommendations are almost equally divided between regulative and non-regulative policy, and the present data refute Salisbury and Heinz's "fundamental hypothesis." That is, assuming that the coalition achieved reflects the costs of achieving the coalition, there is no relationship between coalition and policy type, by level of demand.

The other aspect of the Salisbury and Heinz typology entails using the information costs and the demand system in predicting policy type. High information costs and low demand are proposed to be the most likely concomitants of regulative policy. However, viewing the commissions in terms of the overall index of recommendations (Table 6.2) shows that the Salisbury and Heinz typology does not apply to the present data. The data presented in both tables suggest that the lower demand seems to be more likely to result in regulative policy, but the relationship is not consistent. The decision systems represented by the commissions themselves seem to operate rather independently in arriving at their recommendations.

Actually, the policy outcomes of Salisbury and Heinz are more applicable to what are called policy results—presidential and congressional response—for recommendations are only so much rhetoric and they can be ignored. There is little risk in

Table 6.1

REGULATIVE POLICY VS. NON-REGULATIVE POLICY
BY DEMAND SYSTEM AND ACHIEVED COALITION

			Total
High	Regulative 11	Regulative 7	18
	Non-Regulative 10	Non-Regulative 11	21
DEMAND			
Low	Regulative 12	Regulative 18	30
	Non-Regulative 10	Non-Regulative 16	26
	Not Achieved 43	Achieved 52	95
	COALITION		

saying how things should be, but there are substantial decision costs in making things become what they should be.

Commissioners, like many politicians, engage heartily in the actionless craft of identifying what is wrong with American society and what should be done about the wrongness. Yet, it is clear that there is a surprising level of agreement among the elite and non-elite members of the commissions. Of the 1,269 members, only 104 voiced any public disagreement with recommendations made. The question that remains is not so much what these representative elite and non-elite persons propose as "good," as it is "How can the president and Congress fail to take action in the face of the demands for governmental action?" Certainly, this is a naive question, but it challenges the prevailing notion that elites defend the status quo and suggests that *governmental* elites are obdurate to general demands of any sort, even those made by other elites.

A Presidential commission (one is tempted to generalize) is a pride of domesticated intellectuals and leading intellectuals and leading citizens willing to sacrifice disagreements in hope of

Table 6.2

REGULATIVE POLICY VS. NON-REGULATIVE POLICY
BY DEMAND AND INFORMATION COSTS

							Total
High	Regulative:	1	2	2	1	12	18
	Non-Regulative:	0	1	5	0	15	21
DEMAND							
Low	Regulative:	2	7	5	8	8	30
	Non-Regulative:	3	4	4	9	6	26

Lowest   Highest

Information Costs
(Level of Data-Gathering)

drinking at the springs of power. This hope is a snare and a delusion: the commissarial lions jump to the whip of the politician. And it is the lion tamer whose reputation is enhanced by the lions, not vice versa.[3]

This metaphorical passage fails to note, however, the possibility of the diminution of reputation of both that could occur when other "lions" go unheeded.

Reality

The articulation of demands to the president and to Congress can take on a great variety of forms, but it is rare that demands are expressed as the result of a charge given by the president or by Congress, as is the case with commissions. Possibly, the commissions are ends in themselves, for more than a few have come and gone with no presidential response. However, there is a chance that these advisory bodies take on a life of their own, even to the point of taking seriously the rhetoric that brought them into existence. The next concern is how responsive the president and Congress can be to the demands made by the various sectors represented on commissions in their formulation of recommendations for action.

Although the demand system has not appeared to have much effect in earlier analyses presented, it shows definite effects in sector dominance and information costs (Table 6.3). Policy outcomes, measured by the overall index of recommendations, seemingly are not related to demand, information, or sector. There are links between information costs and recommendations made and the subsequent policy results. In effect, the variables that precede policy outcomes do not appear to be linked by outcomes to results, because, as noted, the recommendations made are independent of practically every reasonable antecedent effect. To persons accustomed to working with interval-level measures, the table must appear to be quite "bare," and it requires some discussion. First, in order to be included in the analyses to follow, a variable had to correlate significantly with other variables. For example, "sector dominance" is significantly correlated with staff size, the use of consultants, coalition, and the ends index; these latter variables are, in turn, highly associated with the level of data gathering. Second, in order to be included in subsequent analyses, each variable was judged on the basis of substantive importance in any test of the typologies and models reviewed earlier. In effect, the process is analogous to the examination of a covariance matrix in analytical factor analysis. The major difference is that, at best, most of the variables employed in the present study are measured at the ordinal level. The nonparametric methods employed do not afford the luxury of "data-dredging," but the methods do permit tests for interaction and spurious relationships.

Table 6.4 illustrates the various combinations of the variables selected in terms of dichotomies and polytomies applied to the variables. The commission types were divided into three categories on the basis of total membership: first, into those commissions dominated by governmental or corporate sector members (twenty-four); second, those commissions dominated by members from the public interest sector

Table 6.3

ZERO-ORDER CORRELATIONS OF SELECTED VARIABLES

	Demand System	Decision System	Information Costs	Results		
	Demand	Sector Dominance	Level of Data Gathering	Outcomes Overall Index	Presidential Support	Legislative Action
Demand						
Sector Dominance	.008+					
Level of Data-Gathering	.0001+	.003+				
Overall Index						
Presidential Support			.046+			
Legislative Action			.097+	.024+	.0000+	

Table 6.4

COMMISSION TYPE, LEVEL OF DATA-GATHERING,
RECOMMENDATION TYPE, AND RESULTS

Commission Type (n)	Data Gathering High	Data Gathering Low	Recommendation Type Regulative	Recommendation Type Non-Regulative	Results None	Results Legislation*	Results Presidential Support	Results Presidential Support plus Legislation
Corporate-Governmental (24)	11	13	4 / 10	7 / 3	1 / 4	/ 1	2 1 / 3	2 5 / 3 2
Public Interest (48)	29	19	13 / 8	16 / 11	4 5 / 4	/ 1	3 3 / 2 3	6 8 / 1 3
Balanced (23)	17	6	10 / 3	7 / 3	4 2 / 1 1	1	2 1	4 4 / 1 2

*Includes 3 commissions of the 9 created by Congress. In these cases, legislation was initiated by Congress.

(forty-eight); and, finally, those commissions characterized by a more-balanced representation of the public interest sector with members of the govenmental and corporate sectors (twenty-three). Level of data gathering was dichotomized on the basis of new research; those commissions reporting the use of newly generated research or research and public hearings were included in the high information costs category, and the other commissions were placed in the low category. Because the overall index of recommendation sets is most representative of the recommendations it was selected for inclusion in the analyses. The overall index was dichotomized into high-manipulability and low-manipulability sets (forty-eight and forty-seven cases, respectively). The categories of results are no action, legislation without presidential support, presidential support with no ensuing legislation (administrative change and/or president's proposing legislation), and presidential support and legislation. It is assumed that the demand system is reflected in the sector dominance and level of data gathering, since the respective zero-order correlations are quite strong. The inclusion of the demand variable per se would have resulted in doubling the number of cells, from forty-eight to ninety-six. Given that the number of cases is ninety-five, the inclusion of the demand variable was considered to be less important than the inclusion of the other variables of interest. Table 6.4 allows a type of "flow-graph" description of the commissions.[4] For example, the corporate-governmental dominated commissions comprised twenty-four of the total sample of ninety-five commissions; thirteen of those commissions used "lower-level" methods of data gathering. Of those thirteen commissions, ten proposed recommendation sets of the more-manipulable type, six of those ten had their recommendations incorporated, in part at least, in a presidential recommendation for legislation. The congressional response was legislation in three of the cases. One obvious observation is that the cell size diminishes quite rapidly as the various combinations are applied.

Information Costs and Policy Type

A method that promises some usefulness in dealing with the

Table 6.5

RELATIVE DIFFERENCES IN PROPORTIONS OF NON-REGULATIVE
RECOMMENDATIONS BY COMMISSION TYPE, BY LEVEL
OF DATA GATHERING (PROPORTION
NON-REGULATIVE)

			Commission Type		
			Corporate-Governmental	Public Interest	Balanced
1)	Level of Data-gathering	Low	.231 (13)	.579 (19)	.500 (6)
		High	.636 (11)	.552 (29)	.412 (17)
2)	d_k		-.405	+.027	+.088
3)	v_i		.018	.030	.083
4)	v_j		.058	.019	.024
5)	v_k		.076	.049	.107
6)	$1/v_k$		13.158	20.408	9.346
7)	w_k		.307	.476	.218
8)	$WK*d_k$		-.124	.013	.019 d=.092
9)	$(d_k-d)^2/v_k$		1.289	2.429	1.682

Chi-square = 5.400
Significance less than .05

small expected cell frequencies is that of maximum-likelihood
and relative differences.[5] It is a general application of
conditional probabilities based upon the changes in the
marginal distributions of variables as they are affected by the
subsequent introduction of other variables and by combinations of variables. Table 6.5 indicates another test of the
Salisbury and Heinz typology, comparing the differences in the
proportions of less-manipulable recommendation sets on the
basis of the level of data gathering, by commission type.
Following Davis's notation,[6] line nine in the table indicates
that there is a significant interaction, that is, significant

differences among the conditional differences, or dk's in line
two (p<.03, >.02). This indicates that the introduction of the
level of data gathering severely skews the marginal proportions
of recommendation types. However, this interaction precludes
the computation of the d-variate, and the relationships cannot
be analyzed in terms of a linear flow graph. For now, it is
sufficient to note that Salisbury and Heinz's notions are
supported. That is, information has a significant effect upon
the type of policy produced by the corporate-governmental
commissions. For those commissions, the higher level of
information costs accompanies a significant, nonadditive
effect, "resulting" in less-manipulable recommendation sets.
Overall, the effects of the level of data gathering are slight (see
Table 6.2); however, corporate-governmental commissions
that conduct more data gathering are more likely to make
recommendations that can be characterized as non-regulative.

Information Costs and Presidential Response

As indicated in Table 6.3, presidential support of commission recommendations is significantly associated with the level
of data gathering. In light of the findings presented in Table
6.5, it will be instructive to examine the relationships between
presidential support, by commission type, and (1) the level of
data gathering and (2) recommendation type. The association
between level of data gathering and presidential support can be
made more clear in terms of Table 6.6. Part A indicates that
governmental and corporate sector–dominated commissions
have used lower levels of data gathering compared with the
public sector–dominated commissions and the balanced
commissions. The proportionate differences, compared with
the public sector commissions are -.1459 for the corporate-
governmental commissions and +.1349 for the balanced commissions. Part B indicates the conditional differences existing
between the level of data gathering and presidential support.
For example, the proportion of corporate-governmental
commissions using higher levels of data gathering is .2937
greater in receiving presidential support than those using
lower-level methods.

The computation of the significance of the differences

appears in parts C and D of Table 6.6. Part C indicates that the effects of the level of data gathering on presidential support are systematic. In general, the level of data gathering on the part of all three types of commissions is higher in those receiving presidential support, but the difference is insignificant. Thus, it may be stated that the zero-order relationship between data gathering and presidential support is spurious. Part D suggests some explanations of the spurious relationship. Compared with all the other commissions, the corporate-governmental commissions generally receive higher presidential support compared with the public interest sector and balanced types of commissions, even after accounting for any effects of the information costs. Coupled with the extremely high level of presidential support of corporate-governmental commissions that conduct more research, these relationships account for most of the variation in presidential response previously accounted for by the higher level of data gathering alone.

Figure 6.1 depicts graphically the relationships described in Table 6.6. The relationships indicated are that the corporate-governmental commissions are less likely to initiate the higher levels of data gathering—as indicated by the arrow from corporate-governmental to "higher level"; the proportionate difference is -.1459 compared with the public interest sector commissions. The direct links between the type of commission and presidential support are indicated by the two arrows labeled .2194 and -.0426 for corporate-governmental commissions and balanced commissions respectively. The "effects" of the higher level of data gathering are indicated by the arrow running from "higher level" to "presidential support."[7] That is, the use of higher levels of data gathering by the corporate-governmental commissions and by the balanced commissions "adds" .2170 to the likelihood of presidential support when compared with the public-dominated commissions. The transmittance of data gathering to the corporate-governmental commissions is only -.0080, practically a negligible effect upon presidential support. That is, the zero-order effect of corporate-governmental commissions' receiving more presidential support is not mediated to any appreciable extent by the level of information. The path from corporate-governmental commis-

Table 6.6

COMMISSION TYPE, LEVEL OF DATA GATHERING
AND PRESIDENTIAL SUPPORT

A. Level of Data-Gathering by Commission Type

Commission Type	Overall Proportion	Level of Data Gathering		N	Difference vs. Public Interest
		High	Low		
Corporate-Governmental	.253	.4583	.5417	24	-.1459
Public Interest	.505	.6042	.3958	48	
Balanced	.242	.7391	.2609	23	+.1349

(Total Proportion High = .6000)

B. Type, Level of Data Gathering and Presidential Support (Proportion Supported)

	High	Low	Difference vs. Low
Corporate-Governmental	.9091 (11)	.6154 (13)	+.2937
Public Interest	.6897 (29)	.4734 (19)	+.2163
Balanced	.6471 (17)	.5000 (6)	+.1471

Difference vs. Public Interest

Corporate-Governmental	+.2194	+.1420
Balanced	-.0426	+.0266

(Proportion Overall Presidential Support = .6421)

C. Differences in Presidential Support by Level of Data Gathering (Proportion Supported)

1) Level of Data Gathering:	High	.9091 (11)	.6897 (29)	.6471 (17)
	Low	.6154 (13)	.4734 (19)	.5000 (6)
2) d_k		+.2937	+.2163	+.1471
3) v_i		.0826	.0238	.0381

Table 6.6 continued

		Corporate Governmental	Public Interest	Balanced
4)	V_j	.0473	.0249	.0833
5)	V_k	.1299	.0487	.1214
6)	$1/V_k$	7.6982	20.4499	8.2372
7)	W_k	.2116	.5620	.2264
8)	W_k*d_k	.0621	.1216	.0333
				d = .2170
9)	$(d_k-d)^2/V_k$	.0453	.0000	.0402
				not significant
10)	d_k^2/V_k	.6640	.9568	.1782
				chi-square = 1.799, not significant
11)	$V_k*W_k^2$	.0058	.0154	.1782
				v = .1655

D. Differences in Presidential Support <u>vs</u>. Public Interest by Level of Data Gathering (Proportion Supported)

			Corporate-Governmental	Balanced
1)	Level of Data Gathering:	High	+.2194 (11)	-.0426 (17)
		Low	+.1420 (13)	+.0266 (6)
2)	d_k		+.0774	-.0692
3)	V_i		.0199	.0025
4)	V_j		.0109	.0044
5)	V_k		.0308	.0069
6)	$1/V_k$		32.4675	144.9275
7)	W_k		.1830	.8170
8)	W_k*d_k		.0142	-.0565
				d = -.0423
9)	$(d_k-d)^2/V_k$		.4652	.0980
				not significant
10)	d_k^2/V_k		.1945	.6940
				chi square = .8885, not significant
11)	$V_k*W_k^2$		.0010	.0046
				v = .0749

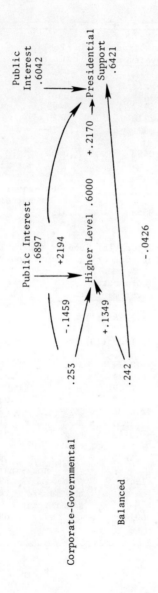

Figure 6.1

FLOW GRAPH OF PRESIDENTIAL SUPPORT BY COMMISSION
TYPE AND LEVEL OF DATA GATHERING

sions direct to presidential support shows the only significant d-value (p = .055). As in Table 6.5 above, the corporate-governmental commissions are different from the other two types; the public interest sector commissions and the more balanced commissions are very similar in regard to the presidential support received.

Policy Type and Presidential Response

Table 6.7 shows a similar pattern for the effects of recommendation type upon presidential support. Part A indicates that corporate-governmental commissions and the balanced commissions are less likely to recommend "risky" policy, compared with the public interest sector commissions. Once again, the high level of presidential support of recommendations made by the corporate-governmental commissions is the overriding consideration. The less-manipulable sets of recommendations are slightly more likely to be associated with presidential support, but the difference is not significant.

Figure 6.2 illustrates the relationships in another way. The slight transmittance of recommendation type, .0997, indicates that recommendation type has little to do with presidential response to commission recommendations.

Another View from the Top

A closer look at the effects of recommendation type, information costs, and commission type upon presidential support can be achieved by the use of "block variables."[8] By using the data given in Table 6.8 and by comparing levels of variables, it is possible to describe the relationship more precisely and, at the same time, compare levels of legislative reaction. The block variables in this application are presidential support and legislative enactment by recommendation type, by level of data gathering. Line 2 of Part A indicates that, for the lower level of data gathering, the less-manipulable recommendation sets supported by the president were generally more likely to result in legislative enactment. The proportional differences for the corporate-governmental com-

Table 6.7

PROPORTIONAL DIFFERENCES BY COMMISSION TYPE,
RECOMMENDATION TYPE AND PRESIDENTIAL SUPPORT

A. Recommendation Type by Commission Type

Commission Type	Overall Proportion	Recommendation Type		N	Difference vs. Public Interest
		Non-Regulative	Regulative		
Corporate-Governmental	.253	.417	.583	24	−.146
Public Interest	.505	.563	.457	48	
Balanced	.242	.435	.575	23	−.128

(Total Proportion Non-Regulative = .4947)

B. Commission Type, Recommendation Type, and Presidential Support (Proportion Supported)

	Non-Regulative	Regulative	Difference vs. Regulative
Corporate-Governmental	.800 (10)	.714 (14)	+.086
Public Interest	.654 (27)	.571 (21)	+.083
Balanced	.700 (10)	.538 (13)	+.162

Difference vs. Public Interest

Corporate-Governmental	+.146	+.143
Balanced	+.046	−.033

(Proportion Overall Presidential Support = .6421)

C. Differences in Presidential Support by Recommendation Type (Proportion Supported)

	Corporate Governmental	Public Interest	Balanced
1) Recommendation Type:			
Non-Regulative	.800 (10)	.654 (27)	.700 (10)
Regulative	.714 (14)	.571 (21)	.538 (13)
2) d_k	+.086	+.083	+.162
3) V_i^k	.0080	.0242	.0700

Table 6.7 continued

4)	V_j	.0510	.0272	.0414
5)	V_k^j	.0590	.0514	.1114
6)	$1/V_k$	16.9492	19.4553	8.9767
7)	W_k	.3735	.4287	.1978
8)	W_k*d_k	.0321	.0356	.0320
				d = .0997
9)	$(d_k-d)^2/V_k$	.0032	.0054	.0353
				not significant
10)	d_k^2/V_k	.1254	.1340	.2356
				chi-square - .4950
				not significant
11)	$V_k*W^2_k$	.0082	.0094	.0044
				v = .1483

D. Difference in Presidential Support vs. Public Interest by Recommendation Type (Proportion Supported)

		Corporate-Governmental	Balanced
1)	Recommendation Type:		
	Non-Regulative	+.146 (10)	+.046 (10)
	Regulative	+.143 (14)	-.035 (13)
2)	d_k	+.003	+.079
3)	V_i	.0146	.0046
4)	V_j	.0102	.0025
5)	V_k^j	.0248	.0071
6)	$1/V_k$	40.3226	140.8451
7)	W_k	.2226	.7774
8)	W_k*d_k	.0007	.0614
			d = .0621
9)	$(d_k-d)^2/V_k$	.1408	.0402
			not significant
10)	d_k^2/V_k	.0038	.8970
			chi-square = .8828
			not significant
11)	$V_k*W_k^2$	.0012	.0043
			v = .0742

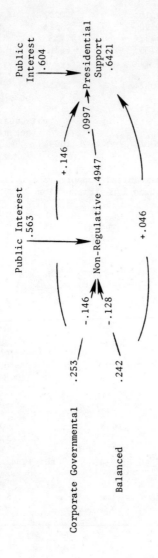

Figure 6.2

FLOW GRAPH OF PRESIDENTIAL SUPPORT BY COMMISSION
TYPE AND RECOMMENDATION TYPE

Table 6.8

BLOCK VARIABLES ANALYSIS, LEGISLATIVE ENACTMENT OF
PRESIDENT-SUPPORTED RECOMMENDATIONS BY TYPE AND
LEVEL OF DATA GATHERING (PROPORTION ENACTED)

A. Low-Level Data Gathering

		Corporate-Governmental	Public Interest	Balanced
1)	Recommendation Type:			
	Non-Regulative	.667 (3)	.273 (11)	.667 (3)
	Regulative	.300 (10)	.167 (8)	.333 (3)
2)	d_k	+.367	+.106	+.334

B. High-Level Data Gathering

		Corporate-Governmental	Public Interest	Balanced
1)	Recommendation Type:			
	Non-Regulative	.714 (7)	.500 (16)	.571 (7)
	Regulative	.500 (4)	.462 (13)	.400 (10)
2)	d_k	+.214	+.038	+.171

missions and the balanced commissions are .367 and .334, respectively; the public interest sector commissions, generally less successful, demonstrate a difference of .106. Part B indicates that a similar pattern exists at the higher level of data gathering, and, quite systematically, the public interest sector recommendations have fared less well than the recommendations of the other two types of commissions. Since the differences illustrated in Part B are somewhat smaller than those in Part A (line 2), there is some indication that higher information costs make an independent contribution to the success of recommendations, regardless of recommendation type, but the small cell sizes preclude any meaningful analysis of this "difference of differences." However, Table 6.8 indicates quite unequivocally the relationships among the type of recommendations, the influence of data gathering, and subsequent actions on the part of the president and Congress.

In each of the blocks of recommendation type and level of data
gathering, the less-manipulable recommendations show higher proportions successful in terms of presidential and legislative support. Moreover, within levels of data gathering, the
more "risky" recommendations are more successful proportionately. Comparing across levels of data gathering, eleven of
the twelve comparisons indicate that the effects of more data are
an increased proportion of successful recommendation sets.
That is, the only proportionately lower success rate for all of
the sets is the .571 proportion for balanced commissions using
higher levels of data gathering, compared with the .667 proportion successful with lower-level information costs.

The Demise of Government by Commission

It would be simple, and simpleminded, to leave the matter
here. The obvious conclusion would be that the corporate-
governmental commissions are the ones that are directed to
muster the greatest research efforts and the ones whose findings
become recommendations that have an easy passage into law
through presidential push. Such, however, is not the case. The
crucial variable that is in operation throughout is the changing
presidential style noted earlier in the documented trends by
administration. Even though the trend toward corporate-
governmental domination of this small slice of the policymaking method continued through the Johnson administration to the Nixon administration, other overriding trends were
those that found commissions less prestigious in their
memberships and less likely to meet with positive presidential
response. So, even though the commission form of "government" came to be the dominion of the corporate representatives, actual policy results from the activities of the later
commissions are practically nil. Table 6.9 shows that a clear
trend toward greater use of commissions' recommendations in
putting items upon the national agenda was broken by Nixon.
Instead of the use of commissions to tap the opinions of elite
groups in general, and of the corporate-governmental elite in
particular, there was a closing off of the inputs that those
representatives might offer to the policymaking process
subsequent to the creation of a commission. This break, which

Table 6.9

PRESIDENTIAL SUPPORT BY ADMINISTRATION

	Presidential Support	
	Does Not Propose Legislation or Support Enacted Legislation	Does Propose Legislation or Support Enacted Legislation
Truman	8	7
Eisenhower	2	6
Kennedy	3	8
Johnson	9	19
Nixon	24	9
TOTAL	46	49

as early as 1970 augured the demise of "government by commission," was acutely evident in 1972. In short, it mattered little which elite or non-elite sector was represented by the commissions, for few actions resulted on the part of the president. Had the trend continued toward corporate domination of the effective commissions, one would have been hard pressed to deny that C. Wright Mills was right in his woeful warnings;[9] they would apply to what became known in the early 1970s as "government by commission"—and government by a nonpublic kind of commission as well.

By this twist, commissions such as those studied here are clearly shown to be but reflections of the man who occupies the office of the President of the United States. They are but extensions of the power of a political actor, tools of his choosing. Most are created by the president, their activities— including the way in which they go about finding the "truth"—are proscribed by the president, and their recommendations of a limited set of possibilities are gleaned by the president for those demands that should be proposed as law. With the narrowing of the participating elites to lower-level members of the corporate sector, no narrowing of alternatives was indicated. The unanswerable question arises: In seeking agreement with his preconceptions, did President Nixon alienate the last elite close to the government? Was this his "high crime and misdemeanor"? As a model, the commission works as a method for arriving at political decisions. As a tradition, the commission, in its own right, may be a legitimate part of the policymaking process. Nixon's breach of the "commission tradition" failed in a most public way. A retrospective view of the Nixon years vitiates the normative view of reality advancing to measure up to rhetoric, and replaces the view with one of rhetoric straining downward toward the level of reality.

Toward More-Public Rhetoric

The Revival of Government and Commissions

For present purposes, the definition of politics may be recast as the management of the disparity between rhetoric and reality. As long as rhetoric continues in the public policy arena, the disparity itself will constitute demands upon the political system. When politicians say nothing publicly, it can be assumed that they do nothing in the public interest, but it cannot be assumed that they do nothing in some narrower interest.

There were notable differences in the use of commissions on the part of the five presidents whose administrations have been studied. In general, commissions came to be more frequent, and they came to be significantly larger in terms of the number of commissioners participating in their activities. Public dissent became a more frequent characteristic of commission proceedings, and presidential response all but disappeared in the Nixon years. Overall, the prestige and representativeness of the commissions declined significantly, they came to be dominated by members representing corporate interests, and participation by the public interest sector declined drastically. If commissions are assumed to reflect changes in the underlying political processes, speculation would indicate that the American policymaking apparatus became less representative of ruling elites in particular, and it became less representative of society in general.

Even with the narrowing of the commissions' representativeness and the emasculation of their role in policymaking, there was no shutting off of the demands that had persisted for over three decades. Heeded or not, the recommendations of the commissions repeated the calls for governmental response to issues that have remained unresolved since 1945. At the least, rhetorical policy survived the shutting down of the government during the Watergate crisis, and, apparently, in January 1977 the government returned to "business as usual."

One of the First Carter Commissions

As promised by his wife in his campaign, one of President Carter's first public actions was the creation of the President's Commission on Mental Health. On February 17, 1977, the president signed Executive Order No. 11973 and charged the commission "to review the mental health needs of the Nation and to make recommendations to the President as to how the Nation might best meet these needs."[1] The commission had Rosalynn Carter as its honorary chairperson. The membership included women; representatives of native American, black, and Mexican-American ethnic minorities; and a former mental patient—a broadly representatvie, non-elite membership.[2]

During its year of operation, the commission held public hearings across the nation and generated thousands of pages of research findings published in four volumes and over thirty task panel reports. The main report made note of earlier commissions and their recommendations while making over one hundred recommendations for action. Most of the recommendations were specific and named the Department of Health, Education, and Welfare as the implementing agency— an administrative approach. However, recommendations also called for congressional appropriation of more funds for mental health programs. The overall tenor of the report was a redistribution of services and a definite, nonincremental increase in services. A major recommendation called for the collaboration of "Federal, State, and local governments" in meeting "the needs of Americans with long-term and servere mental disabilities."[3] In short, this was a highly political report that expressed a strong set of demands upon government.

The commission planned implementation of its recommendations in three ways: short-range implementation through Executive Order; midrange through new initiatives using existing agencies, for example, those joining the Department of Housing and Urban Development and the National Institute of Mental Health in the development of intermediate care facilities; and long-range through congressional initiatives, especially in the area of national health insurance that would include more coverage for mental illness.

The report itself was of special interest to the commissioners who agreed that it should be technically correct, but written in comprehensible language. Foremost in the minds of the commissioners was the broad dissemination of the report to lay and professional audience alike. A considerable amount of effort was spent in making a strong case for each recommendation, and the companion volumes contained nearly two thousand recommendations from which the major recommendations were derived. There was no dissent among the commissioners. All agreed that the first priorities for national action should be directed toward the segments of the population "most in need"—children, youth, the elderly, the chronically mentally ill, and ethnic minorities.

The last official meeting of the commission was characterized by a cautious optimism. The work had been demanding but meaningful. The recommendations made were deemed "possible and realizable," and the call for action was made clearly. However, the commissioners were acutely aware of the lack of response to earlier mental health efforts in the 1960s, and this concern added caution to the meeting. The commissioners discussed the importance of the report's publication being picked up by major newspapers across the country, and they agreed that if this happened, then their efforts would be off to a good start.

After the report was issued in May 1978, President Carter set up a task force reporting to Secretary of Health, Education, and Welfare Joseph Califano. Consisting of officials of the Department of Health, Education, and Welfare, the task force was given the specific charge of implementing the recommendations of the president's commission. As early as the end of 1978, administrative changes had been made, and several pieces of significant legislation had been drafted.[4] Mrs. Carter has continued to play a prominent role in the implementation of the commission's recommendations. In May 1978, she presented the report to a statewide meeting in Texas, and before the end of the year, she had made dozens of presentations in as many states.

Some Positive Signs

Politics in the 1970s will be remembered most for the public arousal so evident throughout the decade. My Lai, Vietnam, Watergate, "Koreagate," the "turnout" of congressional incumbents in 1974 and 1978, the initial popular appeal of President Carter, the Equal Rights Amendment, and California's Proposition 13 brought high public attention to the operations of the president, Congress, and other government entities. The ubiquitous public opinion surveys during these years saw trust in the government range from the lowest point ever recorded to the highest. Some hard lessons were learned that, no matter how short-lived they may be, indicate that the greatest problem facing the American people is not the inadequacy of the government, but the pathology of excessive secrecy in governmental policymaking.[5]

Other early efforts of the Carter administration were aimed at controlling the federal bureaucracy by reducing its size and easing its complicated administrative regulations. The first effort has a dim prognosis, but it continues to nibble away at the "Federal Rathole."[6] The second continues reforms set in motion by the Hoover Commissions of the 1920s. It remains unclear whether "government by administrative discretion" will be controlled.[7] Certainly, none of the findings reported here indicate any lessening of the administrative route toward policy implementation.

In 1975, Senator Kennedy proposed legislation that "would make it a crime for government officials knowingly to lie to or mislead citizens;"[8] not surprisingly, the legislation has not been enacted. However, another Kennedy initiative seems to be finding life in the implementation of the recommendations of President Carter's Commission on Mental Health. Kennedy proposed that, after the issuing of a commission report, the following procedures be followed:

1. The president designates a Cabinet member to be responsible for implementation.
2. The Cabinet member issues a public report within one month of implementation.
3. Six months later, a more-detailed public report indicates the disposition of the commission report, and reasons for the disposition.
4. One year after the commission issues its report, it reconvenes to review the progress made.
5. After two years, the responsible Cabinet member issues a final report on implementation.[9]

Although this approach appears to place severe limitations on the presidential use of the commission method, its intent is quite clear.[10] It is not unreasonable to expect the government to be held accountable for the disparity between rhetoric and reality. Real power is the ability to shape reality;[11] the abuse of power lies in the substitution of empty rhetoric for reality. One possible definition of rhetoric is that of effective communication, and policy commissions may yet prove to be a means of realizing that communication.

Robert L. Sutherland, recounting over forty years of experience as a member of various national commissions and as an observer of many more, noted that presidential advisory commissions serve a great number of purposes. He added the hope that "some day, number one on the list may be the impartial arriving at public policy whose only goal is public well-being."[12] This is a reasonable expectation, for practically every public commission has been given such a goal. Perhaps someday, policymakers will be held strictly accountable for that which they say. Rhetorical policy may not lead directly to action, but rhetorical policy does affect the hopes of those desiring action.

A Final Bow to Reality

There remains the question of what effects are realized by the use of commissions. A certain, circular process is suggested in the sense that the president initiates, empowers, and circumscribes the scope of any commission's activities. That is, the characteristics viewed as "variables" are actually "givens" for any commission. The articulation of a demand, the information costs allocated, and the permissible range of decisions made are highly predictive of the likely results.

The extent to which a commission mirrors the larger, political arena for any issue is problematic. It is difficult to capture the details of recommendations vis-à-vis presidential expectations and presidential support of the "platform" espoused by a commission. Many commissions may well reflect the intent of the president and little else. Nevertheless, the extent to which the public statements of those involved can be "followed" into law and administrative action affords a meaningful description of the policymaking process. The notion of tracing a policy idea through the various stages of reaching the national agenda, legitimation, and implementation is intriguing, as is the determination of subsequent translations of the idea at the legislative level and at the administrative level. Although much present research is directed at the description of the "unintended consequences" of policy, it may be the case that there are fewer unintended outcomes than there are purported to be. That is, given the great diversity of alternatives recommended in commission reports, the notion that policy choices are made from a very limited list of alternative strategies is not strongly supported. Current shortcomings in energy policy, in health care policy, and in the implementation of equal opportunity can hardly be called unintended.

Regardless of arguments about what public policy should be, commissions provide evidence of what policy is not. Few, if any of the commissions created were established to do anyting outside the purview of an existing government entity. However extraordinary the individual circumstances of a commission's role in the formulation of public policy, the frequency and regularity of the use of the commission method demonstrates innate incapabilities on the part of the routinely organized branches of the federal system of government. The same observations may be taken in a positive light as well: some issues and needs may be identified that merit and demand the special processes and public policymaking features unique to public policy commissions.

APPENDIX A:
Presidential Advisory Commissions

Truman Administration (April 12, 1945–Jan. 20, 1953)

1. President's Committee on Integration of the Medical Services of the Government; announced by the president Dec. 12, 1945; report released June 18, 1946; Harold W. Dodds, chairman; "Report to the President of the United States by the Committee on Integration of the Medical Services of the Government" (Press release, June 18, 1946, 9 pp.).

2. National Commission on Higher Education; letter from the president July 13, 1946; report transmitted Dec. 11, 1947; George G. Zook, chairman; *Higher Education for American Democracy*, 6 vols. (Washington, D.C.: Government Printing Office, 1947).

3. President's Advisory Commission on Universal Training; White House announcement Nov. 20, 1946; report dated June 1, 1947; Karl T. Compton, chairman; *Program for National Security* (Washington, D.C.: Government Printing Office, 1947).

4. President's Committee on Civil Rights; Executive Order No. 9808, Dec. 5, 1946; report released Oct. 29, 1947; Charles E. Wilson, chairman; *To Secure These Rights* (Washington, D.C.: Government Printing Office, 1947).

Adapted from Thomas R. Wolanin, *Presidential Advisory Commissions: Truman to Nixon*, © 1975, The University of Wisconsin Press. Used by permission of The University of Wisconsin Press.

5. Advisory Committee on the Merchant Marine; letter to the members March 11, 1947; report made public Nov. 15, 1947; K. T. Keller, chairman; *Report of the President's Advisory Committee on Merchant Marine* (Washington, D.C.: Government Printing Office, 1947).

6. Special Board of Inquiry for Air Safety; letter appointing members June 15, 1947; final report dated Dec. 29, 1947; James M. Landis, chairman; *Report to the President of the U.S.* (Washington, D.C.: Government Printing Office, 1947).

7. President's Committee on Foreign Aid; press release June 22, 1947; report dated Nov. 7, 1947; W. Averell Harriman, chairman; *European Recovery and American Aid* (Washington, D.C.: Government Printing Office, 1947).

8. Air Policy Commission; letter appointing members July 18, 1947; report made public Jan. 13, 1948; Thomas K. Finletter, chairman; *Survival in the Air Age* (Washington, D.C.: Government Printing Office, 1948).

9. President's Water Resources Policy Commission; Executive Order No. 10095, Jan. 3, 1950; report dated Dec. 11, 1950; Morris L. Cooke, chairman; *A Water Policy for the American People, General Report* (Washington, D.C.: Government Printing Office, 1950).

10. President's Communications Policy Board; Executive Order No. 10110, Feb. 17, 1950; report dated Feb. 16, 1951; Irvin Stewart, chairman; *Telecommunications, Program for Progress* (Washington, D.C.: Government Printing Office, 1951).

11. President's Commission on Migratory Labor; Executive Order No. 10129, June 3, 1950; report dated March 26, 1951; Maurice T. Van Hecke, chairman; *Migratory Labor in American Agriculture* (Washington, D.C.: Government Printing Office, 1951).

12. Committee to Review Veterans Hospitals; presidential statement June 5, 1950; report transmitted Sept. 22, 1950; Howard A. Rusk, chairman; *Report to the President on Veterans' Medical Services* (Washington, D.C.: Government Printing Office, 1950).

13. President's Materials Policy Commission; letter to the chairman Jan. 22, 1951; report dated June 2, 1952; William S. Paley, chairman; *Resources for Freedom: A Report to the President*, 5 vols. (Washington, D.C.: Government Printing Office, 1952).

14. President's Commission on the Health Needs of the Nation; Executive Order No. 10317, Dec. 29, 1951; report released Dec. 18, 1952; Paul B. Magnuson, chairman; *Building America's Health*, 5 vols. (Washington, D.C.: Government Printing Office, 1953).

15. Missouri Basin Survey Commission; Executive Order No. 10318, Jan. 3, 1952; report dated Jan. 12, 1953; James E. Lawrence, chairman; *Missouri, Land and Water* (Washington, D.C.: Government Printing Office, 1953).

16. President's Airport Commission; letter to chairman Feb. 20, 1952; report dated May 16, 1952; James H. Doolittle, chairman; *The Airport and Its Neighbors* (Washington, D.C.: Government Printing Office, 1952).

17. President's Commission on Immigration and Naturalization; Executive Order No. 10392, Sept. 4, 1952; report released Jan. 1, 1953; Philip B. Perlman, chairman; *Whom We Shall Welcome* (Washington, D.C.: Government Printing Office, 1953)

Eisenhower Administration (Jan. 20, 1953–Jan. 20, 1961)

18. President's Committee on International Information Activities; statement by the president Jan. 26, 1953; report released July 8, 1953; William H. Jackson, chairman; summary of report appears as White House press release, July 8, 1953, and also in *Department of State Bulletin*, vol. 29 (July 29, 1953).

19. Advisory Committee on Government Housing Policies and Programs; Executive Order No. 10486, Sept. 12, 1953; report issued December 1953; Albert M. Cole, chairman; *Recommendations and Report* (Washington, D.C.: Government Printing Office, 1953).

20. President's Advisory Committee on a National Highway Program; White House announcement Aug. 7, 1954;

report dated January 1955; Lucius D. Clay, chairman; *Ten-Year National Highway Program* (Washington, D.C.: Government Printing Office, 1955).

21. President's Commission on Veterans' Pensions; Executive Order No. 10588, Jan. 14, 1955; report dated April 1956; Omar N. Bradley, chairman; *Findings and Recommendations, Veterans' Benefits in the United States* (Washington, D.C.: Government Printing Office, 1956).

22. President's Committee on Education Beyond High School; PL 84-813, July 26, 1956; final report dated July 1957; Devereux C. Josephs, chairman; *Second Report to the President* (Washington, D.C.: Government Printing Office, 1957). This was the final report of the committee.

23. President's Citizen Advisers on the Mutual Security Program; letter from the president Sept. 22, 1956; report dated March 1, 1957; Benjamin Fairless, chairman; *Report to the President by the President's Citizen Advisers on the Mutual Security Program* (Washington, D.C.: Government Printing Office, 1957).

24. President's Committee to Study the United States Military Assistance Program; letter from the president Nov. 24, 1958; final report transmitted to Congress Aug. 20, 1959; William H. Draper, Jr., chairman; *Composite Report of the President's Committee to Study Military Assistance Program,* 2 vols. (Washington, D.C.: Government Printing Office, 1959).

25. President's Commission on a World's Fair; appointed by the president Oct. 10, 1959; report issued Oct. 29, 1959; Harry A. Bullis, chairman; report was issued as a White House press release, Oct. 29, 1959.

26. Commission on National Goals; White House announcement Feb. 3, 1960; report released Nov. 16, 1960; Henry M. Wriston, chairman; *Goals for Americans* (Englewood Cliffs, N.J.: Prentice-Hall, 1960).

Kennedy Administration (Jan. 20, 1961–Nov. 22, 1963)

27. Panel on Mental Retardation; appointed by the president Oct. 17, 1961; report released Oct. 16, 1962; Leonard

W. Mayo, chairman; *A Proposed Program for National Action to Combat Mental Retardation* (Washington, D.C.: Government Printing Office, 1962).

28. President's Commission on Campaign Costs; Executive Order No. 10974, Nov. 8, 1961; report made public April 18, 1962; Alexander Heard, chairman; *Financing Presidential Campaigns* (Washington, D.C.: Government Printing Office, 1962).

29. President's Committee to Appraise Employment and Unemployment Statistics; statement by the president Nov. 10, 1961; report dated Sept. 27, 1962; Robert A. Gordon, chairman; *Measuring Employment and Unemployment* (Washington, D.C.: Government Printing Office, 1962).

30. President's Commission on the Status of Women; Executive Order No. 10980, Dec. 14, 1961; Eleanor Roosevelt, chairman; *American Women* (Washington, D.C.: Government Printing Office, 1963).

31. President's Advisory Panel on Federal Salary Systems; White House announcement Dec. 28, 1961; final report dated Aug. 16, 1963; Clarence B. Randall, chairman; *Final Report* (Washington, D.C.: Government Printing Office, 1963).

32. President's Council on Pennsylvania Avenue; appointed by the president June 1, 1962; report made public April 1964; Nathaniel A. Owings, chairman; *Pennsylvania Avenue* (Washington, D.C.: Government Printing Office, 1964).

33. Committee on Equal Opportunity in the Armed Forces; letter from the president June 24, 1962; final report released Dec. 28, 1964; Gerhard A. Gesell, chairman; "Initial Report: Equality of Treatment and Opportunity for Negro Military Personnel Stationed within the U.S." (mimeographed, 1963); "Final Report: Military Personnel Stationed Overseas and Participation in the National Guard" (mimeographed, 1964).

34. President's Committee to Strengthen the Security of the Free World; White House announcement Dec. 10, 1962; report released March 22, 1963; Lucius D. Clay, chairman; *The Scope and Distribution of U.S. Military*

and Economic Assistance (Washington, D.C.: Government Printing Office, 1963).

35. President's Advisory Commission on Narcotic and Drug Abuse; Executive Order No. 11076, Jan. 15, 1963; final report released Jan. 24, 1964; E. Barrett Prettyman, chairman: *Final Report* (Washington, D.C.: Government Printing Office, 1963).

36. President's Commission on Registration and Voting Participation; Executive Order No. 11100, March 30, 1963; final report released December 1963; Richard M. Scammon, chairman; *Report of the President's Commission on Registration and Voting Participation* (Washington, D.C.: Government Printing Office, 1963).

37. Committee on Public Higher Education in the District of Columbia; White House announcement Sept. 23, 1963; report released June 1964; Francis S. Chase, chairman; *Report to the President; Public Higher Education in the District of Columbia* (Washington, D.C.: Government Printing Office, 1964).

38. Task Force to Promote Overseas Sale of Securities of U.S. Companies; White House announcement Oct. 2, 1963; report dated April 27, 1964; Henry H. Fowler, chairman; *Report to the President of the U.S.* (Washington, D.C.: Government Printing Office, 1964).

Johnson Administration (Nov. 22, 1963–Jan. 20, 1969)

39. President's Commission on the Assassination of President Kennedy; Executive Order No. 11130, Nov. 29, 1963; report released September 1964; Earl Warren, chairman; *Report* (Washington, D.C.: Government Printing Office, 1964).

40. Commission on Heart Disease, Cancer, and Stroke; announced by the president March 7, 1964; report presented to the president Dec. 9, 1964; Michael E. DeBakey, chairman; *National Program to Conquer Heart Disease, Cancer, and Stroke* (Washington, D.C.: Government Printing Office, 1965).

41. National Commission on Technology, Automation, and Economic Progress; PL 88-444, Aug. 19, 1964; report transmitted to the president Jan. 29, 1966; Howard R. Bowen, chairman; *Technology and the American Economy* (Washington, D.C.: Government Printing Office, 1966).

42. President's Special Panel on Federal Salaries; announced by the president Jan. 28, 1965; report dated April 15, 1965; Marion B. Folson, chairman; *Report* (House Doc. 170, 89th Cong., 1st Sess., 1965).

43. Special Presidential Committee on U.S. Trade Relations with Eastern European Countries and the U.S.S.R.; announced by the president Feb. 16, 1965; report released May 6, 1965; J. Irwin Miller, chairman; *Report to the President* (Washington, D.C.: Government Printing Office, 1965).

44. President's Commission on the Patent System; Executive Order No. 11215, April 8, 1965; report dated Nov. 17, 1966; Harry H. Ransom and Simon Rifkind, cochairmen; *To Promote Progress of Useful Arts in an Age of Exploding Technology* (Washington, D.C.: Government Printing Office, 1966).

45. President's Commission on Crime in the District of Columbia; Executive Order No. 11234, July 16, 1965; report dated Dec. 15, 1966; Herbert J. Miller, chairman; *Report of the President's Commission on Crime in the District of Columbia* (Washington, D.C.: Government Printing Office, 1966).

46. President's Commission on Law Enforcement and Administration of Justice; Executive Order No. 11236, July 23, 1965; report dated February 1967; Nicholas Katzenbach, chairman; *The Challenge of Crime in a Free Society* (Washington, D.C.: Government Printing Office, 1967).

47. National Advisory Commission on Food and Fiber; Executive Order No. 11256, Nov. 4, 1965; report dated July 1967; Sherwood O. Berg, chairman; *Food and Fiber for the Future* (Washington, D.C.: Government Printing Office, 1967).

48. National Advisory Commission on Health Manpower; Executive Order No. 11279, May 7, 1966; report dated Nov. 30, 1967; J. Irwin Miller, chairman, *Report of the National Advisory Commission on Health Manpower* (Washington, D.C.: Government Printing Office, 1967).

49. Presidential Task Force on Career Advancement; announced by the president May 11, 1966; report released spring 1967; John W. Macy, Jr., chairman; *Investment for Tomorrow* (Washington, D.C.: Government Printing Office, 1967).

50. Commission on Marine Science, Engineering, and Resources; PL 89-454, June 17, 1966; report submitted Jan. 11, 1969; Julius A. Stratton, chairman; *Our Nation and the Sea: A Plan for National Action* (Washington, D.C.: Government Printing Office, 1969).

51. National Advisory Commission on Selective Service; Executive Order No. 11289, July 2, 1966; report transmitted to the president February 1967; Burke Marshall, chairman; *In Pursuit of Equity: Who Serves When Not All Serve?* (Washington, D.C.: Government Printing Office, 1967).

52. National Advisory Commission on Libraries; Executive Order No. 11301, Sept. 2, 1966; report transmitted to the president Oct. 3, 1968; Douglas M. Knight, chairman; *Library Services for the Nation's Needs: Toward Fulfillment of a National Policy* (Bethesda, Md.: Educational Resources Information Center, 1968).

53. National Advisory Commission on Rural Poverty; Executive Order No. 11306, Sept. 27, 1966; report dated September 1967; Edward T. Breathitt, chairman; *The People Left Behind* (Washington, D.C.: Government Printing Office, 1967).

54. National Commission on Urban Problems; announced by the president, acting under authority of Sec. 301 of Housing and Urban Development Act of 1965, PL 89-117, Jan. 12, 1967; report issued December 1968; Paul H. Douglas, chairman; *Building the American City* (Washington, D.C.: Government Printing Office, 1968).

55. President's Commission on Budget Concepts; announced by the president March 3, 1967; report dated Oct. 10, 1967; David M. Kennedy, chairman; *Report of the President's Commission on Budget Concepts* (Washington, D.C.: Government Printing Office, 1967).

56. President's Commission on Postal Organization; Executive Order No. 11341, April 8, 1967; report dated June 1968; Frederick R. Kappel, chairman; *Towards Postal Excellence* (Washington, D.C.: Government Printing Office, 1968).

57. President's Committee on Urban Housing; presidential directive June 3, 1967; report issued Jan. 1, 1969; Edgar F. Kaiser, chairman; *A Decent Home* (Washington, D.C.: Government Printing Office, 1969).

58. National Advisory Commission on Civil Disorders; Executive Order No. 11365, July 29, 1967; report dated March 1, 1968; Otto Kerner, chairman; *Report of the National Advisory Commission on Civil Disorders* (Washington, D.C.: Government Printing Office, 1968).

59. Commission on Obscenity and Pornography; PL 90-100, Oct. 3, 1967; report released Sept. 30, 1970; William D. Lockhart, chairman; *The Report of the Commission on Obscenity and Pornography* (Washington, D.C.: Government Printing Office, 1970).

60. National Advisory Commission on Health Facilities; appointed by the president Oct. 6, 1967; report issued December 1968; Boisfeuillet Jones, chairman; *Report to the President* (Washington, D.C.: Government Printing Office, 1968).

61. Industry-Government Special Task Force on Travel; appointed by the president Nov. 16, 1967; report issued February 1968; Robert M. McKinney, chairman; *Report to the President of the U.S.* (Washington, D.C.: Government Printing Office, 1968).

62. National Commission on Product Safety; PL 90-146, Nov. 20, 1967; report dated June 1970; Arnold Elkind, chairman; *Final Report of the National Commission on Product Safety* (Washington, D.C.: Government Printing Office, 1970).

63. President's Commission on Income Maintenance Pro-

gram's; presidential directive Jan. 2, 1968; report dated Nov. 12, 1969; Ben W. Heineman, chairman; *Poverty Amid Plenty: The American Paradox* (Washington, D.C.: Government Printing Office, 1969).

64. President's Commission for the Observance of Human Rights Year, 1968; Executive Order No. 11394, Jan. 20, 1968; final report transmitted to the president April 29, 1969; W. Averell Harriman, chairman; *To Continue Action for Human Rights, Final Report* (Washington, D.C.: Government Printing Office, 1969).

65. National Commission on the Causes and Prevention of Violence; Executive Order No. 11412, June 10, 1968; report transmitted to the president Dec. 10, 1969; Milton Eisenhower, chairman; *To Establish Justice, To Insure Domestic Tranquility* (Washington, D.C.: Government Printing Office, 1969).

66. Committee on Population and Family Planning; announced by the president July 16, 1968; report transmitted to the president Jan. 7, 1969; Wilbur J. Cohen and John D. Rockefeller III, cochairmen; *Population and Family Planning: Transition from Concern to Action* (Washington, D.C.: Government Printing Office, 1968).

Nixon Administration, First Term
(Jan. 20, 1969–Jan. 20, 1973)

67. President's Commission on an All-Volunteer Armed Force; announced by the president March 27, 1969; report submitted Feb. 20, 1970; Thomas S. Gates, chairman; *Report* (Washington, D.C.: Government Printing Office, 1970).

68. President's Advisory Council on Executive Organization; announced by the president April 5, 1969;termination announced May 7, 1971; Roy Ash, chairman; *A New Regulatory Framework* (Washington, D.C.: Goverment Printing Office, 1971).

69. Presidential Task Force on International Development; announced in presidential message to Congress May 28,

1969; report submitted March 4, 1970; Rudolph A. Peterson, chairman; *U.S. Foreign Assistance in the 1970s: A New Approach* (Washington, D.C.: Government Printing Office, 1970).

70. President's Task Force on Business Taxation; announced by the president Sept. 22, 1969; report dated September 1970; John H. Alexander, chairman; *Business Taxation* (Washington, D.C.: Government Printing Office, 1970).

71. President's Task Force on Improving the Prospects of Small Business; announced by the president Sept. 24, 1969; report presented Dec. 1, 1969; J. Wilson Newman, chairman; *Improving the Prospects of Small Business* (Washington, D.C.: Government Printing Office, 1970).

72. President's Task Force on Model Cities; announced by the president Sept. 24, 1969; report transmitted Dec. 16, 1969; Edward C. Banfield, chairman; *Model Cities: A Step Towards the New Federalism* (Washington, D.C.: Government Printing Office, 1970).

73. President's Task Force on Rural Development; announced by the president Sept. 29, 1969; report transmitted Jan. 12, 1970; Mrs. Haven Smith, chairman; *A New Life for the Country* (Washington, D.C.: Government Printing Office, 1970).

74. President's Task Force on Women's Rights and Responsibilities; announced by the president Oct. 1, 1969; report submitted Dec. 15, 1969; Virginia R. Allan, chairman; *A Matter of Simple Justice* (Washington, D.C.: Government Printing Office, 1970).

75. President's Task Force on Higher Education; announced by the president Oct. 6, 1969; report submitted Jan. 15, 1970; James M. Hester, chairman; *Priorities in Higher Education* (Washington, D.C.: Government Printing Office, 1970).

76. President's Task Force on Science Policy; announced by the president Oct. 6, 1969; report presented Dec. 10, 1969; Ruben F. Mettler, chairman; *Science and Technology; Tools for Progress* (Washington, D.C.: Government Printing Office, 1970).

77. President's Task Force on Low Income Housing;

announced by the president Oct. 10, 1969; report submitted Jan. 15, 1970; Raymond J. Saulnier, chairman; *Toward Better Housing for Low Income Families* (Washington, D.C.: Government Printing Office, 1970).

78. President's Task Force on the Aging; announced by the president Oct. 10, 1969; report presented Feb. 20, 1970; Garson Meyer, chairman; *Toward a Brighter Future for the Elderly* (Washington, D.C.: Government Printing Office, 1970).

79. President's Task Force on Oceanography; announced by the president Oct. 10, 1969; report submitted Dec. 18, 1969; James H. Wakelin, Jr., chairman: *Mobilizing to Use the Seas* (Washington, D.C.: Government Printing Office, 1970).

80. President's Task Force on the Physically Handicapped; announced by the president Oct. 15, 1969; report transmitted Feb. 10, 1970; Ralph E. DeForest, chairman; *A National Effort for the Physically Handicapped* (Washington, D.C.: Government Printing Office, 1970).

81. President's Task Force on Economic Growth; announced by the president Oct. 15, 1969; report submitted Jan. 9, 1970; Neil H. Jacoby, chairman; *Policies for American Economic Progress in the Seventies* (Washington, D.C.: Government Printing Office, 1970).

82. President's Task Force on Prisoner Rehabilitation; announced by the president Oct. 16, 1969; report submitted Jan. 27, 1970; John M. Briley, chairman; *The Criminal Offender—What Should Be Done?* (Washington, D.C.: Government Printing Office, 1970).

83. President's Task Force on Urban Renewal; announced by the president Oct. 17, 1969; report submitted Jan. 12, 1970; Miles L. Colean, chairman; *Urban Renewal: One Tool among Many* (Washington, D.C.: Government Printing Office, 1970).

84. President's Task Force on Highway Safety; announced by the president Oct. 23, 1969; report submitted December 1969; Franklin M. Kreml, chairman; *Mobility without Mayhem* (Washington, D.C.: Government Printing Office, 1970).

85. President's Task Force on Air Pollution; announced by the president Nov. 18, 1969; report submitted June 9, 1970; Arie Jan Haagen-Smit, chairman; *Cleaner Air for the Nation* (Washington, D.C.: Government Printing Office, 1970).

86. President's Task Force on the Mentally Handicapped; announced by the president Dec. 18, 1969; report submitted May 28, 1970; Jeannette Rockefeller, chairman; *Action Against Mental Disability* (Washington, D.C.: Government Printing Office, 1970).

87. President's Commission on School Finance; Executive Order No. 11513, March 3, 1970; final report submitted March 3, 1972; Neil H. McElroy, chairman; *Schools, People, and Money: The Need for Educational Reform* (Washington, D.C.: Government Printing Office, 1972).

88. President's Panel on Nonpublic Education; announced by the president April 21, 1970; report submitted April 14, 1972; Clarence Walton, chairman; *Nonpublic Education and the Public Good* (Washington, D.C.: Government Printing Office, 1972).

89. Commission on International Trade and Investment Policy; appointment of members announced by the president May 21, 1970; report dated July 1971; Albert L. Williams, chairman; *United States International Economic Policy in an Interdependent World* (Washington, D.C.: Government Printing Office, 1971).

90. President's Commission on Campus Unrest; Executive Order of June 13, 1970; report transmitted Sept. 26, 1970; William W. Scranton, chairman; *Report* (Washington, D.C.: Government Printing Office, 1970).

91. President's Commission on Financial Structure and Regulation; appointment of members announced by the president June 16, 1970; report submitted Dec. 22, 1972; Reed O. Hunt, chairman; *Report* (Washington, D.C.: Government Printing Office, 1972).

92. President's Commission for the Observance of the Twenty-fifth Anniversary of the United Nations; Executive Order No. 11546, July 9, 1970; report submitted April 26, 1971; Henry Cabot Lodge, chair-

man; *Report* (Washington, D.C.: Government Printing Office, 1971).

93. President's Commission on Federal Statistics; announced by the president August 12, 1970; report submitted Sept. 25, 1971; W. Allen Wallis, chairman; *Federal Statistics* (Washington, D.C.: Government Printing Office, 1971).

94. Commission on American Shipbuilding; PL 91-464, Oct. 21, 1970; report submitted Oct. 19, 1973; Albert G. Mumma, chairman; *Report* (Washington, D.C.: Government Printing Office, 1973).

95. National Commission on Materials Policy; PL 91-512, Oct. 26, 1970; report transmitted June 27, 1973; Jerome L. Klaff, chairman; *Material Needs and the Environment Today and Tomorrow* (Washington, D.C.: Government Printing Office, 1973).

96. National Commission on State Workmen's Compensation Laws; PL 91-596, Dec. 29, 1970; report submitted July 31, 1972; John F. Burton, Jr., chairman; *Report* (Washington, D.C.: Government Printing Office, 1972).

97. President's Advisory Panel on Timber and the Environment; appointment of members announced by the president Sept. 2, 1971; report submitted April 30, 1973; Fred A. Seaton, chairman; *Report* (Washington, D.C.: Government Printing Office, 1973).

98. President's Committee on Health Education; appointment of chairman announced Dec. 29, 1971; report presented Sept. 25, 1973; R. Heath Larry, chairman; *Report* (Washington, D.C.: Department of Health, Education, and Welfare; Health Services and Mental Health Administration, n.d.).

99. Presidential Study Commission on International Radio Broadcasting; announced by the president Aug. 10, 1972; report submitted Feb. 5, 1973; Milton S. Eisenhower, chairman; *The Right to Know* (Washington, D.C.: Government Printing Office, 1973).

APPENDIX B:
Coding Procedure

For ninety-three of the ninety-nine commissions created during the period under investigation, reports were published and disseminated by the United States Government Printing Office or by some other government agency. Four other reports were issued as press releases; the report of the Commission on National Goals, *Goals for Americans*, was published by the American Assembly; and the report of the Committee on Equal Opportunity in the Armed Forces, "the Gesell Report," was made public in a relatively unusual manner. The initial Gesell Report was originally mimeographed and classified as "secret." However, since the report was the subject of a heated congressional debate, it was made public before the usual declassification period had elapsed. In fact, it appeared in its complete form in the *Congressional Record* of August 7, 1963, within days of the president's receiving the report.

Four reports were not available for use in the present study. Of the four reports issued as press releases, only one, the report of the President's Committee on International Information Activities, is available in its complete form in the *Department of State Bulletin* of July 29, 1953. Three other reports issued as press releases are available only as summary statements appearing in various editions of *Published Papers of the Presidents;* they are probably to be found in the millions of papers and other documents stored in presidential libraries, although they do not appear in catalogs of such papers. These three commissions, not represented in the present sample, are: President's Committee on Integration of the Medical Services of the Government (1945-1946), Special Board of Inquiry for Air Safety (1947), and the President's Commission on a World's Fair (1959). The fourth report not available for the present study is that of the President's Council on Pennsylvania Avenue (1962-1964); due to a cataloging error, the report was not sent to government depositories in time to be used.

A considerable time lag occurs between the reporting of findings to the president and to Congress and the subsequent placing of the documents in government depositories. Since presidential response and legislative actions related to a commission's recommendations are included in the analysis of the commission, reports issued after February 1973 are not included in the present study.

Locating recommendations in the text of each report was aided by the relatively consistent formats of the reports. Numbering, use of italics or boldface print, summaries, and page references in tables of contents or indexes made the location of recommendations relatively easy; only a small number of reports required thorough reading of each page to find the recommendations. To increase the consistency of locating and coding the recommendations, ten commission reports were selected at random for content analysis. Five judges were assigned the task of locating the statements in the text of each of the ten reports. The location was identified by page number, line number, and key words or complete statements. Even though differing degrees of difficulty in locating the recommendations were reported, each judge agreed upon the location of recommendations in 255 out of the 270 statements listed. The remaining fifteen were located by at least three of the five judges. Those three became the coders for the remainder of the study, although the bulk of the coding operations fell to two of them. Random checks of consistency were made during the coding process, and the reports were coded in a random order to afford checks against biasing effects. None was found. However, it was discovered subsequently that the average number of statements per report was fifty-three, a considerably larger number than had been found in the random sample of reports. This finding did not suggest the injection of any bias into the coding protocol and resulted from a handful of reports with exeedingly numerous recommendations. These lengthier reports were, on the whole, the ones that offered the greatest ease of locating recommendations because of their formats. With a high degree of certainty, it can be stated that most of the recommendations were located for use in the analysis to follow.

Each of the 270 statements located in the manner described was identified by its report and order in the text and keypunched verbatim on IBM cards. Using Hewitt and Amsler's *Basic Text-Processing Programs* (1976), and excluding from the counting procedure indefinite articles and some prepositions, a 4,300-word glossary was produced. Of the total number of words, 1,845 occurred only once. A more interesting feature of the glossary was the listing of more than 50 words with a frequency of occurrence of 10 to 96 times. Table B-1 gives a list of the most frequently occurring words in the ten-commission sample. High on the list are "should" and "recommends/recommendation." Obviously, these words are characteristic of the commissions' nature. Of even higher importance are the frequent occurrences of words such as "legislation," "act," "provide," "establish," "president," "states," "agencies," "federal," and "planning." The frequently occurring words were then entered into a "concordance" program to determine the co-occurrence of modal word types (Hewitt and Amsler, 1976). The joint frequencies, which appeared as complete statements ordered on the basis of the words selected, were examined for patterns and for differentiation among homonyms (Kelley and Stone, 1975). Definite patterns were found, and these became the basis for the coding of the recommendations of the remaining eighty-five commission reports. Figure B-1 gives an example of the concordance of the words "state" and "legislation."

Initially, a set of decision rules was developed for the classification of statements by computer. These rules followed generally the disambiguation techniques of Stone et al. (1966) and of Kelley and Stone (1975), but the rules became so complex that the processing capacity of the computer was not sufficient for even the relatively simpler tasks. Several simplifying programs were developed to ease the strain upon the data-

Table B-1

MOST-FREQUENT WORDS IN TEN-COMMISSION SAMPLE

Word	Frequency	Word	Frequency
Act	13	Funding	11
Action(-s)	10	Government(-s)	
Agencies	17	Governmental	37
Amend		Health	64
Amended		Housing	38
Amendment(-s)	17	Improve(-d)	
Appropriate		Improvements	11
Appropriations	13	Income(-s)	15
Area(-s)	12	Increase(-d)	
Authorize		Increasing	11
Authorization	10	Information	11
Budget	15	Laws	14
Commission(-s)		Legislate(-d)	
Committee(-s)	36	Legislation	
Community(-ies)	12	Legislature(-s)	13
Comprehensive	16	Local	
Congress	10	Localities	
Construction	13	Locally	14
Cost	15	Nation(-al)	17
Develop(-ed)		New(-ly)	11
Development	24	Plan(-s)	
Discriminate		Planning	28
Discrimination		President	12
Discriminatory	11	Private(-ly)	11
Economic	12	Program(-s)	38
Education(-al)	27	Provide(-d)	
Effective	11	Provisions	44
Employ		Public	19
Employment	21	Recommend(-s)	
Establish(-ed)		Recommendation	52
Establishment	18	Rights	14
Expand(-ed)		School(-s)	
Expansion	10	Schooling	15
Expenditure	10	Services	25
Facility(-ies)	31	Should	96
Family(-ies)	13	State(-s)	41
Federal(-ly)	51	Support(-s)	14
Financing	10	System(-s)	18
Fund(-s)		Training	15
Funded		Women	28

```
                                              STATE LEGISLATION
, APPLICABLE TO BOTH MEN AND WOMEN, SHOULD BE ENACTED
AND EXTENDED TO ALL TYPES OF EMPLOYMENT, TO PROVIDE MINI
MUM WAGE        LEVELS APPROXIMATING THE MINIMUM UNDER F
EDERAL LAW AND TO REQUIRE        PREMIUM PAY AT THE RATE
OF AT LEAST TIME AND A HALF FOR OVERTIME.
          UNTIL SUCH TIME AS THIS GOAL IS ATTAINED, STATE LEGISLATION
LIMITING  MAXIMUM HOURS OF WORK FOR WOMEN SHOULD BE M
AINTAINED, STRENGTHENED,    AND EXPANDED.
```

Figure B-1

CONCORDANCE OF "STATE" AND "LEGISLATION"

processing central memory unit, but whenever data entry exceeded two thousand words of text the combinations and permutations became astronomical. For this reason, it was necessary to employ human coders for the larger number of recommendation statements. A useful product of the computer analysis was a complete list of 270 recommendations which proved invaluable for subsequent checks upon coder reliability.

The rudimentary categories provided by the computer-assisted content analysis were modified to include other modal words and words that could be reasonably expected to belong in the respective categories. The words were sorted into three categories on the basis of actor (grammatically, the subject of the statement), action (the verbs), and ends (the adverbial clauses or modifiers). Subclassifications were developed for each category—actor, action, ends—and the coding protocol took on its final form. Categories, subclassifications, and keywords are presented in Table 4.1 in Chapter 4.

While this coding protocol seems to be cumbersome, it was reliable in practice, although somewhat tedious. For the original sample of ten commission reports, the five judges coded the 270 recommendations that had been content analyzed, along with 40 other recommendations from commissions that were not included in the sample study. Recommendations were coded by each judge, both in the original context of the report and in the form of discrete, randomly ordered statements. Reliability was assessed by noting the extent to which the judges agreed totally in the three-digit codes assigned to each statement. Complete consistency was achieved in over 90 percent of the coding operations. The residual classifications showed very complicated inconsistencies. No relevant patterns were found among the judges, except that there appeared to be an effort to make the vague categories "fit" into less-vague categories. This phenomenon was markedly less evident when the recommendations were coded from their original context; this suggests that the judges read for information outside the physical confines of the statements.

However, since the ultimate coding of recommendations was done with the recommendations in context and in random order of commission reports, it is to be assumed that no significant biasing of coding resulted. Periodic checks of inter-rater reliability found the agreement among judges to be at or above 90 percent. If any bias exists in the ultimate codes, it is toward making vague codes less vague, a point of some subsequent importance. As a matter of course, commission reports with ten or fewer recommendations were coded by two judges, and complete agreement between the two judges was achieved in every case.

Notes

Technical Note

No doubt some readers will wonder about the use of statistical significance reporting with a decidedly nonrandom sample. As a teacher of statistics, the author does know better, but I provide the following rationale. First, the overriding interest in using statistics is in describing the phenomena; for this reason, the significance levels indicate a degree of relationship more adequately than mere numbers. Second, of high interest is the conceptual fit of notions about policy models in general; thus, statistics that indicate the direction and strength of relationships are used, but they are used in the spirit of construct validation. Third, many other studies of the policymaking process have seen fit to use such statistics with other, nonrandom samples. As Blalock observes,

> We turn, briefly, to certain situations in which nonprobability sampling has been used. The major disadvantage of nonprobability sampling is that we can obtain no valid estimate of our risks of error. Therefore, statistical inference is not legitimate and should not be used. This does not mean that nonprobability sampling is never appropriate. In exploratory studies, the main goal of which is to obtain valuable insights which ultimately may lead to testable hypotheses, probability sampling either may be too expensive or lead to fewer such insights. . . . The fact that you can undoubtedly think of studies in which statistical tests have been made on such extreme cases does not mean that such a procedure is legitimate. This is not to deny, however that useful insights may be obtained by such a comparison. (Hubert M. Blalock, Jr., *Social Statistics*, 2d. ed. [New York: McGraw-Hill, 1972], pp. 527-28).

The author, however, takes sole responsibility for the decision made.

Chapter 1

1. James N. Danziger, "Comparing Approaches to the Study of Financial Resource Allocation," in *Comparative Public Policy: Issues, Theories, and Methods*, ed. Craig Liske, William Loehr, and John McCamant (New York: Wiley, 1975), p. 55; Thomas R. Dye, *Politics, Economics and the Public: Policy Outcomes in the American States* (Chicago: Rand McNally, 1966), pp. 1-19. Danziger, Dye, and numerous other policy scientists treat fully the problem of defining "policy." Both Danziger and Dye express appreciation of the intangible effects of policy: Danziger writes of a political system as "the institutions and processes which authoritatively allocate public values" (p. 55); Dye states "policy outcomes express the value allocations of a society, and these allocations are the chief output of the society's political system" (p. 1). I read these definitions to include connotations that the term "values" has for the disciplines of sociology, psychology, and economics; I accept the ironic twist that this implies—some public policy might be intended to change public perceptions of what is to be "valued." The theme of "rhetoric and reality" is not whimsical alliteration; it is, rather, a theme underlying questions about who makes what kinds of plans for which types of actions in the interest of what "public."

2. Bertram M. Gross, "The State of the Nation: Social Systems Accounting" in *Social Indicators*, ed. Raymond A. Bauer (paperback ed., Cambridge: M.I.T. Press, 1966), p. 155.

3. U.S. Commission on Civil Rights, *Federal Civil Rights Enforcement Efforts: A Reassessment* (Washington, D.C.: Government Printing Office, 1973); U.S. Congress, Senate Committee on Labor and Public Welfare, Hearings before the Subcommittee on Children and Youth, *American Families: Trends and Pressures, 1973* (Washington, D.C.: Government Printing Office, 1973); U.S. Department of Health, Education, and Welfare, *Health: United States 1975* (Rockville, Md.: Public Health Service, 1976). For pithier reading, see any issue of *Declassified Documents Quarterly News* (Arlington, Va.: Carrolton Press, 1975—).

4. Randall B. Ripley, "Policy-Making: A Conceptual Scheme," in Randall B. Ripley and Grace A. Franklin, eds., *Policy-Making in the Federal Executive Branch* (New York: Free Press, 1975), pp. 1-20.

5. Ripley, pp. 10-11.

6. Ira Sharkansky, ed., *Policy Analysis in Political Science* (Chicago: Markham Publishing Co., 1970), p. 1.

7. Ripley, pp. 11-12.

8. Nick Kotz, *Let Them Eat Promises: The Politics of Hunger in America* (Garden City, N.Y.: Doubleday and Co., 1971); James D. Barber, *Citizen Politics: An Introduction to Political Behavior* (Chicago: Markham Publishing Co., 1969); James S. Coleman, "The Concept of Equality of Educational Opportunity," *Harvard Educational Review* 38 (Winter 1968):7-22; Harold L. Wilensky, *The Welfare State and Equality: Structural and Ideological Roots of Public Expenditures* (Berkeley: University of California Press, 1975).

9. Joseph Schumpeter, *Capitalism, Socialism, and Democracy* (London: George Allen & Unwin, 1943), p. 242.

10. David Easton, *A Systems Analysis of Political Life* (New York: John Wiley, 1965), Chapter 1.

11. Robert Salisbury and John Heinz, "A Theory of Policy Analysis and Some Preliminary Applications," in *Policy Analysis in Political Science*, ed. Ira Sharkansky (Chicago: Markham Publishing Co., 1970), pp. 39-60.

12. Thomas R. Dye and L. Harmon Zeigler, *The Irony of Democracy: An Uncommon Introduction to American Politics* (Belmont, Calif.: Wadsworth Publishing Co., 1970), p. 257.

13. Samuel Eliot Morison, *The Oxford History of the American People* (New York: Oxford University Press, 1965), p. 1121.

14. Dye and Zeigler, pp. 230-36.

15. Donald Lambro, *The Federal Rathole* (New Rochelle, N.Y.: Arlington House Publishers, 1975), pp. 173-200.

16. Max Weber, *From Max Weber: Essays in Sociology*, trans. Hans Gerth and C. Wright Mills (New York: Oxford University Press, 1946); Aaron Wildavsky, "The Political Economy of Efficiency: Cost-Benefit Analysis, Systems Analysis, and Program Budgeting," *Public Administration Review* 26 (1966):292-310.

17. Richard M. Cyert and James G. March, *A Behavioral Theory of the Firm* (Englewood Cliffs, N.J.: Prentice-Hall, 1963), p. 122; Peter Bachrach and Morton S. Baratz, "Decisions and Non-Decisions," *American Political Science Review* 57 (September 1963):632-42; Frederick C. Dyer and John M. Dyer, *Bureaucracy vs. Creativity* (Coral Gables, Fla.: University of Miami Press, 1965).

18. Dye and Zeigler, pp. 236-40.

19. *United States Constitution*, Article II, Section 3.

20. Ripley and Franklin, pp. 182-84; Dye and Zeigler, pp. 240-42.

21. James M. Burns and Jack W. Peltason, *Government by the People: The Dynamics of American National Government*, 5th ed. (Englewood Cliffs, N.J.: Prentice-Hall, 1963), pp. 378-82; Thomas R. Wolanin, *Presidential Advisory Commissions: Truman to Nixon*

(Madison, Wis.: University of Wisconsin Press, 1975), p. 8.

22. Thomas R. Wolanin, *Presidential Advisory Commissions: 1945-1968* (Ann Arbor, Mich.: University Microfilms, 1973), pp. 16-17.

23. Frank Popper, *The President's Commissions* (New York: Twentieth Century Fund, 1970), pp. 4-7; Wolanin, 1975, p. 7.

24. Popper, p. 56; Wolanin, 1973, p. 275.

25. Daniel Bell, "Government by Commission," *The Public Interest* 3 (Spring 1966):3-9; Popper, p. 56; Anthony M. Platt, *The Politics of Riot Commissions: 1917-1970* (New York: Macmillan Co., 1971), p. 21; Ray C. Rist, "Polity, Politics, and Social Research: A Study in the Relationship of Federal Commissions and Social Science," *Social Problems* 21, no. 1 (Summer 1973):113-28; Michael Lipsky and David J. Olson, *Commission Politics: The Processing of Racial Crisis in America* (New Brunswick, N.J.: Transaction Books, 1977).

26. Harold L. Wilensky, *Organizational Intelligence: Knowledge and Policy in Government and Industry* (New York: Basic Books, 1967), p. 3; Ira Sharkansky, *The Routines of Politics* (New York: Van Nostrand Reinhold Co., 1970).

27. Thomas R. Dye, *Who's Running America? Institutional Leadership in the United States* (Englewood Cliffs, N.J.: Prentice-Hall, 1976, pp. 191-96).

Chapter 2

1. Frank Popper, *The President's Commissions* (New York: Twentieth Century Fund, 1970), p. 6: "Since 1945, commissions have remained important sources of advice. . . . Presidents have also used other means to obtain unbiased advice. . . . But none of these advisory mehanisms are really comparable to the presidential commission. None are so prestigious, none involve such massive effort, none deal with such broad problems, and none so publicly advise the President. Indeed, no other advisory mechanisms of the American government can be considered a true alternative to the presidential commission."

2. Thomas R. Wolanin, *Presidential Advisory Commissions: 1945-1968* (Ann Arbor, Mich.: University Microfilms, 1973), p. 120.

3. Thomas R. Dye, *Who's Running America? Institutional Leadership in the United States* (Englewood Cliffs, N.J.: Prentice-Hall, 1976), pp. 197-203.

4. Wolanin, pp. 119-20.

5. Reymundo Rodriguez, member of the President's Commission on Mental Health (1977-1978), personal communication.

6. Walter White, *A Man Called White* (New York: Viking Press, 1948), pp. 329-32.

7. Wolanin, pp. 120-21.

8. Bertram M. Gross, "The State of the Nation: Social Systems Accounting," in *Social Indicators*, ed. Raymond A. Bauer (paperback ed., Cambridge: M.I.T. Press, 1966), p. 155.

9. Wolanin, pp. 210-34.

10. Executive Order No. 11234, Office of the President, 1965.

11. Wolanin, p. 143.

12. Wolanin, pp. 144-47.

13. Commission on National Goals, *Goals for Americans* (Englewood Cliffs, N.J.: Prentice-Hall, 1960), p. vi.

14. Wolanin, p. 152.

15. Commission on Obscenity and Pornography, *Report of the Commission on Obscenity and Pornography*, ed. Clive Barnes (New York: New York Times Publishing Co., 1970), p. 595.

16. Robert Salisbury and John Heinz, "A Theory of Policy Analysis and Some Preliminary Applications," in *Policy Analysis in Political Science*, ed. Ira Sharkansky (Chicago: Markham Publishing Co., 1970), pp. 39-60.

17. Salisbury and Heinz, p. 43.

18. *Goals for Americans*, pp. 24-33.

19. Commission on International Trade and Investment Policy, *United States International Economic Policy in an Interdependent World* (Washington, D.C.: Government Printing Office, 1971), pp. 311-88.

20. *Report of the Commission on Obscenity and Pornography*, p. 518.

21. Ibid., pp. 517-18.

22. *Published Papers of the Presidents* (Washington, D.C.: Government Printing Office, 1970), p. 940.

23. Presidential Study Commission on International Radio Broadcasting, *The Right to Know* (Washington, D.C.: Government Printing Office, 1973), p. v.

24. President's Commission on Campaign Costs, *Financing Presidential Campaigns* (Washington, D.C.: Government Printing Office, 1962), p. iv.

Chapter 3

1. Thomas R. Dye, *Who's Running America? Institutional Leadership in the United States* (Englewood Cliffs, N.J.: Prentice-Hall, 1976); G. William Domhoff, *Who Rules America?* (Englewood

Cliffs, N.J.: Prentice-Hall, 1967); Thomas R. Dye and L. Harmon Zeigler, *The Irony of Democracy: An Uncommon Introduction to American Politics* (Belmont, Calif.: Wadsworth Publishing Co., 1970).

2. Dye, p. 14 (his emphasis).

3. Thomas R. Wolanin, *Presidential Advisory Commissions: 1945-1968* (Ann Arbor, Mich.: University Microfilms, 1973), p. 331.

4. Anthony M. Platt, *The Politics of Riot Commissions* (New York: Macmillan Co., 1971), p. 21; Frank Popper, *The President's Commissions* (New York: Twentieth Century Fund, 1970), p. 56; Dye, pp. 192-96.

5. Dye, p. 14.

6. Dye, pp. 13-14.

7. For all references to commission reports, see Appendix A.

Chapter 4

1. Robert Salisbury and John Heinz, "A Theory of Policy Analysis and Some Preliminary Applications," in *Policy Analysis in Political Science*, ed. Ira Sharkansky (Chicago: Markham Publishing Co., 1970), pp. 39-60; Randall B. Ripley, "Policy-Making: A Conceptual Scheme," in Randall B. Ripley and Grace A. Franklin, eds., *Policy-Making in the Federal Executive Branch* (New York: Free Press, 1975), pp. 1-20 (esp. fn. p. 20). The most common policy measure used is *expenditures*, but we are concerned with policy actions prior to budget time. See also, James N. Danziger, "Comparing Approaches to the Study of Financial Resource Allocation," in *Comparative Public Policy: Issues, Theories, and Methods*, ed. Craig Liske, William Loehr, and John McCamant (New York: Wiley, 1975), pp. 55-85; and Donald T. Allensworth, *The U.S. Government in Action: Public Policy and Change* (Pacific Palisades, Calif.: Goodyear Publishing Co., 1972).

2. Thomas R. Dye and L. Harmon Zeigler, *The Irony of Democracy: An Uncommon Introduction to American Politics* (Belmont, Calif.: Wadsworth Publishing Co., 1970), p. 333.

3. Salisbury and Heinz, pp. 47-49.

4. Ibid., pp. 54-55.

5. Ripley, pp. 16-17; Lance T. LeLoup, "Agency Policy Actions: Determinants of Nonincremental Change," in Ripley and Franklin, pp. 65-90.

6. Executive Order No. 9808, *Establishing the President's Committee on Civil Rights*, 1946.

7. Executive Order No. 10129, *Establishing the President's Commission on Migratory Labor*, 1950.

8. Executive Order No. 10486, *Providing for the Establishment of the Advisory Committee on Government Housing Policies and Programs*, 1953.

9. President's Task Force on Women's Rights and Responsibilities, *A Matter of Simple Justice* (Washington, D.C.: Government Printing Office, 1970), p. ix.

10. President's Advisory Commission on Universal Training, *Program for National Security* (Washington, D.C.: Government Printing Office, 1947).

11. President's Commission on Crime in the District of Columbia, *Report of the President's Commission on Crime in the District of Columbia* (Washington, D.C.: Government Printing Office, 1966).

12. Advisory Committee on Government Housing Policies and Programs, *Recommendations and Report* (Washington, D.C.: Government Printing Office, 1953), p. 19.

13. Dye and Zeigler, p. 333.

14. Yvonne M. Bishop, Stephen E. Fienberg, and Paul W. Holland, *Discrete Multivariate Analysis: Theory and Practice* (Cambridge: M.I.T. Press, 1975), pp. 33-47.

15. Steven A. Shull, "The Relationship between Budgetary and Functional Policy Actions," in Ripley and Franklin, pp. 111-13.

16. Ripley, p. 20 (fn.).

17. Thomas R. Dye, *Who's Running America? Institutional Leadership in the United States* (Englewood Cliffs, N.J.: Prentice-Hall, 1976), p. 15 (his emphasis); obviously, compromise is an important part of the agreement process. For a fascinating, objective discussion of "the art of compromise" see Thomas V. Smith, *A Non-Existent Man: An Autobiography* (Austin, Tex.: University of Texas Press, 1962), especially pp. 109-14.

Chapter 5

1. Thomas R. Wolanin, *Presidential Advisory Commissions: Truman to Nixon* (Madison, Wis.: University of Wisconsin Press, 1975), pp. 133-39 and 216-45. Wolanin provides excellent, exhaustive information pertaining to the impact of commissions. His complex scheme for coding presidential support and government action (see esp. pp. 138-39) makes use of nonexclusive, qualitatively scaled categories of support and action. These were modified somewhat for the present application. In the present use, policy results are defined

as positive presidential response, administrative action, and legislative enactment, whether "minor" or "significant." Actions that did not occur within approximately four years of the publication of a commission's final report are not included (p. 281, note 10).

2. Lance T. LeLoup and Steven A. Shull, "Congress Versus the Executive: The 'Two Presidencies' Revisited," *Social Science Quarterly* 59 (March 1979):704-19.

3. LeLoup and Shull; Aaron Wildavsky, "The Two Presidencies," *Transaction* 4 (1966):449.

4. Thomas R. Wolanin, *Presidential Advisory Commissions: 1845-1968* (Ann Arbor, Mich.: University Microfilms, 1973), pp. 280-81.

5. President's Task Force on Women's Rights and Responsibilities, *A Matter of Simple Justice* (Washington, D.C.: Government Printing Office, 1970), p. v.

6. In response to the recommendations of civil rights, Public Law 80-886, 62 Stat. 1231, July 2, 1948, was passed. It pertains to the evacuation claims of Japanese-Americans, and it is, at most, only remotely related to civil rights; see Wolanin, 1975, p. 217. There was no response at all to the Commission on National Goals.

7. Thomas E. Cronin and Sanford D. Greenberg, eds., *The Presidential Advisory System* (New York: Harper and Row, 1969); Harold L. Wilensky, *Organizational Intelligence: Knowledge and Policy in Government and Industry* (New York: Basic Books, 1967), esp. Chapter 5; Randall B. Ripley and Grace A. Franklin, eds., *Policy-Making in the Federal Executive Branch* (New York: Free Press, 1975).

8. President's Commission on the Health Needs of the Nation, *Building America's Health* (Washington, D.C.: Government Printing Office, 1952), p. 3.

9. Ibid., p. 38.

10. Ibid., p. 54.

11. Ibid., p. 60.

12. President's Commission on Immigration and Naturalization, *Whom We Shall Welcome* (Washington, D.C.: Government Printing Office, 1953), p. xv.

13. Ibid., p. 263.

14. Ibid., p. 265.

15. Commission on National Goals, *Goals for Americans* (Englewood Cliffs, N.J.: Prentice-Hall, 1960), p. 1.

16. Ibid., p. 4.

17. National Advisory Commission on Rural Poverty, *The People Left Behind* (Washington, D.C.: Government Printing Office, 1967), p. 18.

18. Ibid., p. 19.

19. Ibid.

20. President's Materials Policy Commission, *Resources for Freedom*, vol. 1, *Foundations for Growth and Security* (Washington, D.C.: Government Printing Office, 1952), pp. 127-30.

21. Wolanin, 1973, p. 418.

22. National Commission on Materials Policy, *Material Needs and the Environment Today and Tomorrow* (Washington, D.C.: Government Printing Office, 1973), p. R-9.

Chapter 6

1. Robert Salisbury and John Heinz, "A Theory of Policy Analysis and Some Preliminary Applications," in *Policy Analysis in Political Science*, ed. Ira Sharkansky (Chicago: Markham Publishing Co., 1970), p. 43.

2. Ibid.

3. William Lehman, "Crime, the Public and the Crime Commission: A Critical Review of the Challenge of Crime in a Free Society," *Michigan Law Review* 66 (May 1968):1489.

4. James A. Davis, "Analyzing Contingency Tables with Linear Flow Graphs: D Systems," in David R. Heise, ed., *Sociological Methodology 1976* (San Francisco: Jossey-Bass, 1976), pp. 111-45.

5. Ibid.; also Leo A. Goodman, "A Modified Multiple Regression Approach to the Analysis of Dichotomous Variables," *American Sociological Review* 37 (February 1972):28-46.

6. Davis, p. 127.

7. Ibid., p. 136.

8. Ibid., pp. 132-38.

9. C. Wright Mills, *The Power Elite* (New York: Oxford University Press, 1959), pp. 360-61. Although Mills centered his concern on the ascendancy of the military, his general thesis was: "The men of the higher circles are not representative men; their high position is not a result of moral virtue, their fabulous success is not firmly connected with meritorious ability. Those who sit in the seats of the high and mighty are selected and formed by the means of power, the sources of wealth, the mechanics of celebrity, which prevail in their society" (p. 361).

Chapter 7

1. President's Commission on Mental Health, *Report to the President from the President's Commission on Mental Health*, vol. 1 (Washington, D.C.: Government Printing Office, 1978), p. i.

2. Ibid., p. ii; also personal interview with Reymundo Rodriguez, member of the President's Commission on Mental Health (1977-1978).

3. President's Commission on Mental Health, p. 22.

4. Reymundo Rodriguez, personal interview.

5. Harold L. Wilensky, *Organizational Intelligence: Knowledge and Policy in Government and Industry* (New York: Basic Books, 1967), pp. 175-81.

6. Dennis Farney, "Carter Fighting a Losing Battle against Commissions," *Wall Street Journal*, May 27, 1977, p. 1. The use of the word *commission* is in its broadest sense and includes none of the public commissions in the present sample. Among others, however, the Condor Advisory Commission was eliminated.

7. Clark C. Havighurst, *Administrative Discretion: Problems of Decision-Making by Governmental Agencies* (Dobbs Ferry, N.Y.: Oceana Publications, 1974). Those who think that the need to study "administrative law" is passé should read this timely book.

8. Gwynn Nettler, *Explaining Crime*, 2nd ed. (New York: McGraw-Hill, 1978), p. 12.

9. Thomas R. Wolanin, *Presidential Advisory Commissions: Truman to Nixon* (Madison, Wis.: University of Wisconsin Press, 1975), p. 197.

10. Ibid., pp. 197-98.

11. Peter L. Berger and Thomas Luckmann, *The Social Construction of Reality: A Treatise in the Sociology of Knowledge* (Garden City, N.Y.: Doubleday and Company, Anchor Books, 1967), p. 109.

12. Robert L. Sutherland, personal communication, September 9, 1976.

Bibliography

Allensworth, Donald T. *The U.S. Government in Action: Public Policy and Change.* Pacific Palisades, Calif.: Goodyear Publishing Co., 1972.

Alwin, Duane F. "Approaches to the Interpretation of Relationships in the Multitrait-Multimethod Matrix." In *Sociological Methodology 1973-1974*, edited by Herbert L. Costner. San Francisco: Jossey-Bass, 1974.

Bachrach, Peter, and Baratz, Morton S. "Decisions and Non-Decisions." *American Political Science Review* 57 (September 1963):632-42.

Barber, James D. *Citizen Politics: An Introduction to Political Behavior.* Chicago: Markham Publishing Co., 1969.

Barnes, Clive, ed. *Report of the Commission on Obscenity and Pornography.* Washington, D.C.: U.S. Government Printing Office, 1970. New York: New York Times Publishing Co., 1970.

Bauer, Raymond A., and Gergen, Kenneth J. *The Study of Policy Formation.* New York: Free Press, 1968.

Becker, Theodore, ed. *The Impact of Supreme Court Decisions.* New York: Oxford University Press, 1963.

Bell, Daniel. "Government by Commission." *Public Interest* 3 (Spring 1966):3-9.

Berger, Peter L., and Luckmann, Thomas. *The Social Construction of Reality: A Treatise in the Sociology of Knowledge.* New York: Doubleday, 1966.

Bishop, Yvonne M.; Finenberg, Stephen E.; and Holland,

Paul W. *Discrete Multivariate Analysis: Theory and Practice.* Cambridge, Mass.: M.I.T. Press, 1975.

Blalock, Hubert M., Jr. *Social Statistics.* 2d ed. New York: McGraw-Hill, 1972.

Blau, Peter M. *The Dynamics of Bureaucracy.* 2d ed. Chicago: University of Chicago Press, 1963.

Bottenberg, R. A., and Christal, R. E. "Grouping Criteria— A Method Which Retains Maximum Predictive Efficiency." *Journal of Experimental Education* 36 (Summer 1968):28-54.

Burns, James M., and Peltason, Jack W. *Government by the People: The Dynamics of American National Government.* 5th ed. Englewood Cliffs, N.J.: Prentice-Hall, Inc., 1963.

Caputo, David A. *Politics and Public Policy in America.* Philadelphia: J. B. Lippincott Co., 1974.

Carney, T. F. *Content Analysis: A Technique for Systematic Inference from Communication.* Manitoba: University of Manitoba Press, 1972.

Carzo, Rocco, and Yanouzas, John N. *Formal Organization: A Systems Approach.* Homewood, Ill.: Richard D. Irwin, Inc., and Dorsey Press, 1967.

Charlesworth, James C. *Contemporary Political Analysis.* New York: Free Press, 1967.

Cherns, A. B.; Sinclair, R.; and Jenkins, W. I. *Social Science and Government: Policies and Problems.* London: Tavistock Publications, 1972.

Christ, Carl. *Econometric Models and Methods.* New York: John Wiley & Sons, Inc., 1966.

Christal, R. E. "Selecting a Harem—and Other Applications of the Policy Capturing Model." *Journal of Experimental Education* 36 (Summer 1968):35-41.

Cole, Arthur Harrison. *A Finding-List of British Royal Commission Reports.* Cambridge, Mass.: Harvard University Press, 1935.

Coleman, James S. "The Concept of Equality of Educational Opportunity." *Harvard Educational Review* 38 (Winter 1968):7-22.

_____. *Policy Research in the Social Sciences.* Morristown, N.J.: General Learning Press, 1972.

Cronin, Thomas E., and Greenberg, Sanford D., eds. *The Presidential Advisory System.* New York: Harper and Row, 1969.

Cyert, Richard M., and March, James G. *A Behavioral Theory of the Firm.* Englewood Cliffs, N.J.: Prentice-Hall, Inc., 1963.

Danziger, James N. "Comparing Approaches to the Study of Financial Resource Allocation." In *Comparative Public Policy: Issues, Theories, and Methods,* edited by Craig Liske, William Loehr, and John McCamant. New York: John Wiley, 1975.

Davis, James, Jr., and Dolbeare, Kenneth M. "Selective Service and Military Manpower: Induction and Deferment Policies in the 1960s." In *Political Science and Public Policy,* edited by Austin Ranney. Chicago: Markham Publishing Co., 1968.

Davis, James A. "Hierarchical Models for Significance Tests in Multivariate Contingency Tables: An Exegesis of Goodman's Recent Papers." In *Sociological Methodology: 1973-1974,* edited by Herbert L. Costner. San Francisco: Jossey-Bass, 1974.

_____. "Analyzing Contingency Tables with Linear Flow Graphs: D Systems." In *Sociological Methodology 1976,* edited by David R. Heise. San Francisco: Jossey-Bass, 1976.

Demerath, N. J., III; Larson, Otto; and Schuessler, Karl F. *Social Policy and Sociology.* New York: Academic Press, 1975.

Derthick, Martha. "On Commissionship—Presidential Variety." *Public Policy* 19 (Fall 1971):625.

Dolbeare, Kenneth M., ed. *Political Change in the United States: A Framework for Analysis.* New York: McGraw-Hill Book Co., 1974.

_____. *Public Policy Evaluation.* Beverly Hills: Sage, 1975.

Domhoff, G. William. *Who Rules America?* Englewood Cliffs, N.J.: Prentice-Hall, 1967.

Dye, Thomas R. *Politics, Economics, and the Public: Policy Outcomes in the American States.* Chicago: Rand McNally, 1966.

———. *Understanding Public Policy.* Englewood Cliffs, N.J.: Prentice-Hall, 1972.

———. *Who's Running America? Institutional Leadership in the United States.* Englewood Cliffs, N.J.: Prentice-Hall, 1976.

Dye, Thomas R., and Zeigler, L. Harmon. *The Irony of Democracy: An Uncommon Introduction to American Politics.* Belmont, Calif.: Wadsworth Publishing Co., 1970.

Dyer, Frederick C., and Dyer, John M. *Bureaucracy vs. Creativity.* Coral Gables, Fla.: University of Miami Press, 1965.

Easton, David. *The Political System: An Inquiry into the State of Political Science.* New York: Alfred Knopf, 1953.

———. *A Framework for Political Analysis.* Englewood Cliffs, N.J.: Prentice-Hall, 1965.

———. *A Systems Analysis of Political Life.* New York: John Wiley, 1965.

Farney, Dennis. "Carter Fighting a Losing Battle against Commissions." *Wall Street Journal,* May 27, 1977, p. 1.

Fligner, Michael A., and Wolfe, Douglas A. "Some Applications of Sample Analogues to the Probability Integral Transformation and a Coverage Property." *American Statistician* 30 (May 1976):78-84.

Fowler, Edmund P., and Lineberry, Robert L. "Comparative Policy Analysis and the Problems of Reciprocal Causation." In *Comparative Public Policy: Issues, Theories, and Methods,* edited by Craig Liske, William Liehr, and John McCamant. New York: John Wiley, 1975.

Froman, Lewis A. *Congressmen and Their Constituencies.* Chicago: Rand McNally, 1963.

———. "An Analysis of Public Policies in Cities." *Journal of Politics* 29 (February 1976):94-108.

Glaser, Barney G., and Strauss, Anselm L. *The Discovery of Grounded Theory.* Chicago: Aldine, 1967.

Goodman, Leo A. "A Modified Multiple Regression Approach to the Analysis of Dichotomous Variables." *American Sociological Review* 37 (February 1972):28-46.

_____. "A General Model for the Analysis of Surveys." *American Journal of Sociology* 77 (May 1972):1035-88.

Graglia, Lino. *Disaster by Decree*. Ithaca, N.Y.: Cornell University Press, 1976.

Gross, Bertram M. "The State of the Nation: Social Systems Accounting." In *Social Indicators*, edited by Raymond H. Bauer. Cambridge, Mass.: M.I.T. Press, 1966.

Hall, Richard H. *Organizations: Structure and Process*. Englewood Cliffs, N.J.: Prentice-Hall, 1971.

Havighurst, Clark C. *Administrative Discretion: Problems of Decision-Making by Governmental Agencies*. Dobbs Ferry, N.Y.: Oceana Publications, 1974.

Hewitt, Helen-Jo, and Amsler, Robert A. *Basic Text-Processing Programs: A Manual*. Austin, Tex.: Humanities Research Center, 1976.

Hofferbert, Richard I. "Ecological Development and Policy Change." *Midwest Journal of Political Science* 10 (November 1966). Reprinted in Ira Sharkansky, ed. *Policy Analysis in Political Science*. Chicago: Markham Publishing Co., 1970.

Holmes, William M. "Social Conditions and Policy Change." In Randall B. Ripley and Grace A. Franklin, eds. *Policy-Making in the Federal Executive Branch*. New York: Free Press, 1975.

Holsti, Oli R. *Content Analysis for Social Science and Humanities*. Reading, Mass.: Addison-Wesley, 1969.

Hoover, Herbert. *The Memoirs of Herbert Hoover: 1920-33*. New York: Macmillan, 1952.

Johnston, John. *Econometric Methods*. New York: McGraw-Hill, 1963.

Kelley, H. H., and Thibaut, J. W. "Experimental Studies of Group Problem Solving and Process." In *Handbook of Social Psychology*, Volume 2, edited by Gardner Lindzey. Cambridge: Addison-Wesley, 1954.

Kelly, Edward, and Stone, Philip. *Computer Recognition of English Work and Senses*. Amsterdam: North-Holland, 1975.

Kotz, Nick. *Let Them Eat Promises: The Politics of Hunger in America.* Garden City, N.Y.: Doubleday and Co., 1971.

Lambro, Donald. *The Federal Rathole.* New Rochelle, N.Y.: Arlington House Publishers, 1975.

Lehman, William. "Crime, the Public, and the Crime Commission: A Critical Review of the Challenge of Crime in a Free Society." *Michigan Law Review* 66 (May 1968):1487-1540.

LeLoup, Lance T. "Agency Policy Actions: Determinants of Nonincremental Change." In Randall B. Ripley and Grace A. Franklin, eds. *Policy-Making in the Federal Executive Branch.* New York: Free Press, 1975.

LeLoup, Lance T., and Shull, Steven A. "Congress Versus the Executive: The 'Two Presidencies' Revisited." *Social Science Quarterly* 59 (March 1979):704-19.

Lifson, Melvin W. "Value Theory." In *Cost Effectiveness: Economic Evaluation of Engineered Systems*, edited by J. Morley English. New York: John Wiley, 1968.

Lipsky, Michael, and Olson, David J. "Riot Commission Politics." *Transaction* 6 (July/August 1969):8-21.

Lowi, Theodore. "American Business, Public Policy, Case Studies and Political Theory." *World Politics* 16 (July 1964):677-715.

March, James G., ed. *Handbook of Organizations.* Chicago: Rand McNally, 1965.

March, James G., and Simon, Herbert. *Organizations.* New York: John Wiley, 1958.

Marcy, Carl M. *Presidential Commissions.* New York: King's Crown Press, 1945.

Mills, C. Wright. *The Power Elite.* New York: Oxford University Press, 1959.

Morison, Samuel Eliot. *The Oxford History of the American People.* New York: Oxford University Press, 1965.

Nettler, Gwynn. *Explaining Crime*, 2d. ed. New York: McGraw-Hill, 1978.

Perrow, Charles. *Complex Organizations: A Critical Essay.* Glenview, Ill.: Scott, Foresman and Co., 1971.

Platt, Anthony M. *The Politics of Riot Commissions: 1917-1970.* New York: Macmillan Co., 1971.

Popper, Frank. *The President's Commissions.* New York: Twentieth Century Fund, 1970.

Published Papers of the President: The Nixon Years, 1968-72. Washington, D.C.: U.S. Government Printing Office, 1973.

Ripley, Randall B., and Franklin, Grace A., eds. *Policy-Making in the Federal Executive Branch.* New York: Free Press, 1975.

Rist, Ray C. "Polity, Politics, and Social Research: A Study in the Relationship of Federal Commissions and Social Science." *Social Problems* 21 (Summer 1973):113-28.

Rose, Arnold M. *Theory and Method in the Social Sciences.* Minneapolis: University of Minnesota Press, 1954.

Rossi, Peter; Berk, Richard; and Eidson, Betty. *The Roots of Urban Discontent: Public Policy, Municipal Institutions, and the Ghetto.* New York: John Wiley & Sons, 1974.

Salisbury, Robert, and Heinz, John. "A Theory of Policy Analysis and Some Preliminary Applications." In Ira Sharkansky, ed. *Policy Analysis in Political Science.* Chicago: Markham Publishing Co., 1970.

Schumpeter, Joseph. *Capitalism, Socialism, and Democracy.* London: George Allen & Unwin, 1943.

Shapiro, Martin. *Law and Politics in the Supreme Court: New Approaches to Political Jurisprudence.* New York: Free Press, 1964.

Sharkansky, Ira, ed. *Policy Analysis in Political Science.* Chicago: Markham Publishing Co., 1970.

_____. *The Routines of Politics.* New York: Van Nostrand Reinhold Co., 1970.

Shull, Steven A. "The Relationship between Budgetary and Functional Policy Actions." In Randall B. Ripley and Grace A Franklin, eds. *Policy-Making in the Federal Executive Branch.* New York: Free Press, 1975.

Siegel, Sidney. *Nonparametric Statistics for the Behavioral Sciences.* New York: McGraw-Hill, 1956.

Smith, Thomas V. *A Non-Existent Man: An Autobiography.* Austin, Tex.: University of Texas Press, 1962.

Stone, Philip J.; Dunphy, Dexter C.; Smith, Marshall, S.; and Daniel M. Ogilvie and Associates. *The General*

Inquirer: A Computer Approach to Content Analysis.
Cambridge, Mass.: M.I.T. Press, 1966.

U.S., Commission on Civil Rights. *Federal Civil Rights Enforcement: A Reassessment.* Washington, D.C.: Government Printing Office, 1973.

U.S., Congress, Senate Committee on Labor and Public Welfare, Subcommittee on Children and Youth. *American Families: Trends and Pressures, 1973.* Washington, D.C.: Government Printing Office, 1973.

U.S., Department of Health, Education, and Welfare. *Health: United States 1975.* Rockville, Md.: Public Health Service, 1976.

Van Gigch, John P. *Applied General Systems Theory.* New York: Harper & Row, 1974.

Weber, Max. *From Max Weber: Essays in Sociology.* Translated by Hans Gerth and C. Wright Mills. New York: Oxford University Press, 1946.

White, Walter. *A Man Called White.* New York: Viking Press, 1948.

Wildavsky, Aaron. "The Political Economy of Efficiency: Cost-Benefit Analysis, Systems Analysis, and Program Budgeting." *Public Administration Review* 26 (1966): 292-310.

Wilensky, Harold L. *Organizational Intelligence: Knowledge and Policy in Government and Industry.* New York: Basic Books, 1967.

_____. *The Welfare State and Inequality: Structural and Ideological Roots of Public Expenditures.* Berkeley: University of California Press, 1975.

Wolanin, Thomas R. *Presidential Advisory Commissions: 1945-1968.* Ann Arbor, Mich.: University Microfilms, 1973.

_____. *Presidential Advisory Commissions: Truman to Nixon.* Madison, Wis.: University of Wisconsin Press, 1975.

Index

Administrative discretion, 118, 152 n. 7

Advisory bodies. *See* Commissions

Aging, President's Task Force on, 42, 75, 77

Air Policy Commission, 75

Airport Commission, President's, 42

Allen, Virginia R., 41, 56

All-Volunteer Armed Force, President's Commission on an, 27

Assassination of President Kennedy, President's Commission on the (Warren Commission), 18-19, 80

Breathitt, Edward, 42

Califano, Joseph, 117

Campaign Costs, President's Commission on, 33

Campus Unrest, President's Commission on, 19

Carter, James E., 18, 116-118

Carter, Rosalynn, 116, 118

Civil Disorders, National Advisory Commission on, 19

Civil Rights, President's Committee on, 18, 19, 77, 80

Commissions, public; activities of, 16; alternatives in policymaking, 17, 146 n. 1; characteristics of, 11-12; creation of, methods for, 19-23; creation of, reasons for, 17-23; definition of, 11-13; functions of, 12, 16; research conducted by, 28-29; staffs of, 26-27; success of 77-80. *See also* Policymaking; Policy models; Policy outputs; Policy results

Congress; failure of, 83-87; policy actor, role as 6-10; policy initiator, role as, 10; policy recommendations, response to, 66-67; manipulability of, 69. *See also* Policymaking; Policy models; Policy outputs; Policy results

Constitution, U.S., and president's powers, 6, 10

Crime in the District of Columbia, President's Commission on, 32, 58

Crisis (crises), governmental responses to, 10-11

Davis, James A., 101

DeBakey, Michael E., 41

Decision costs; defined, 31-33; relationship with other variables, 89-91. *See also* Policymaking; Policy models; Policy process

Demands; defined, 1-2; variations in, 23. *See also* Policymaking; Policy models; Policy process

Doolittle, James H., 41